HARLEY-DAVIDSON MUSEUM® MASTERPIECES

Dain Gingerelli

Photography by Randy Leffingwell

1934

motorbooks

First published in 2010 by Motorbooks, an imprint of MBI Publishing Company, 400 First Avenue North, Suite 300, Minneapolis, MN 55401 USA

The information in this book is true and complete to the best of our knowledge. All recommendations are made without any guarantee on the part of the author or Publisher, who also disclaims any liability incurred in connection with the use of this data or specific details.

We recognize, further, that some words, model names, and designations mentioned herein are the property of the trademark holder. We use them for identification purposes only.

Motorbooks titles are also available at discounts in bulk quantity for industrial or sales-promotional use. For details write to Special Sales Manager at MBI Publishing Company, 400 First Avenue North, Suite 300, Minneapolis, MN 55401 USA.

To find out more about our books, visit us online at www.motorbooks.com.

Library of Congress Cataloging-in-Publication Data
Gingerelli, Dain, 1949-
  Harley-Davidson Museum masterpieces / Dain Gingerelli ; photographs, Randy Leffingwell.
     p. cm.
  Includes index.
  ISBN 978-0-7603-3894-0 (pbk. : alk. paper)
 1. Harley-Davidson motorcycle—Catalogs. 2. Harley-Davidson Museum—Catalogs. 3. Harley-Davidson motorcycle—History. I. Leffingwell, Randy, 1948- II. Title.
  TL448.H3G53 2010
  629.227'5—dc22

                                                                                          2010014130

Editor: Darwin Holmstrom
Design Manager: Kou Lor
Layout by: Kazuko Collins
Cover designed by: John Sticha

Printed in China

Published by Motorbooks, an imprint of MBI Publishing Company, under license from Harley-Davidson Motor Company.

On the frontispiece and title page: 1934 Model VLD.

On the front cover: 1948 Model FL.

On the back cover, top: 1928 Model JH. **Center:** 1971 Model FX Super Glide. **Bottom:** 1990 Fat Boy.

CONTENTS

INTRODUCTION

So there I was during the summer of 1971, an eager, somewhat brash 22-year-old trying to launch a new FX Super Glide (above) off the line at Lion's Drag Strip in Long Beach, California. Standing nearby were two of the best motorcycle drag racers of their time, Mel "Dish" Disharoon and Leo Payne. Both men drag raced Harleys, and they knew how to ride them fast through the quarter-mile. It had been only a few days since I was hired on as Technical Editor for a new and fledgling publication, *Hot Bike* magazine, and the publisher sent Dish and Leo to observe (read: help) my technique.

Now, I was not a newbie to drag racing—I had won more than my share of street races aboard my Hondas and a Suzuki that I later road raced—so it wasn't like I was being thrown mercilessly into the deep end of the pool. But launching a bike with a small-bore, high-revving engine is different than prompting a Harley off the line. That big ol' American engine likes to build up steam at a more leisurely pace, so coordinating throttle and clutch required a slightly different technique than I was used to with my rice burners. Long story short, I finally harnessed the Glide for some respectable runs through the lights.

But I took back more than just a few impressive timing slips to the office that afternoon. Leo and Dish also taught me how to treat each motorcycle individually, one from the other; to give each motorcycle its due respect. In short, as riders and enthusiasts, it's our job to adapt to the bike; don't expect the bike to conform to your wants and needs.

And thus began my long relationship with Harley-Davidson motorcycles: My first magazine road test was of a 1972 XLCH (for *Hot Bike*), my christening aboard a custom bike was on a chopper with a Shovelhead engine and a front end that stretched into the next time zone (for *Street Chopper*), and the first sidecar I ever piloted—and rode in—was strapped to a 1979 FLH (for *Cycle Guide* magazine). To say that I've been blessed with one of the best jobs a bike enthusiast can ask for is an understatement.

Since that first launch down Lion's magical Armco gauntlet in 1971 I've been editor for four national magazines that cater to Harley enthusiasts. Along the way I've met some interesting Harley owners and industry wags, and I've gained insight into the psyche of what makes Harley owners tick. I also have a deeper appreciation for bikes that wear the Bar & Shield logo, so when I was asked to author this book, I felt honored, and somewhat flattered. It was like a mini homecoming for me, and the journey to complete the chapters about the 50 Harleys reacquainted me with many of the same bikes that I had either ridden or been exposed to at shows, events, or races in the past 40 years.

When people learn that I write for Harley magazines, the first thing they typically ask is, "what's your favorite Harley?" Before answering, I think back to that afternoon at the drag strip with Dish and Leo, and so I qualify my forthcoming answer with an explanation: "Each Harley is different from the others. So you really can't lump them into one category." And then I proceed to explain which models do more to excite me than do others.

Having said that, I should probably point out a few of my favorite Harleys, starting with the current models. I've always been a

fan of the Heritage Softail (above) because it mixes the nostalgic styling that floats my boat with the forceful ride that you expect from a Big Twin. And for pounding out the miles for a cross-country ride, any Electra Glide will do, with a Road King variation taking a close second on my list.

I currently own a 2006 XL that I'm converting into a café racer—sort of a Dain G.'s version of Willie G.'s original 1977 XLCR—but my favorite Sportster-powered model is the XR-1200, although the XR-750 is even more special to me. I'm also a fan of the original XLR, even though some purists claim that model was not a bona fide Sportster. No matter, it's a cool bike.

You can't argue with the nostalgic cool of a Knucklehead, either, and no engine grabs the eye like a Panhead. While we're in that era, the WL (and the WR race variant) and K (and its KR racing cousin) score sky-high on my list, too.

Since we're soiling the soles of our shoes on the dirt tracks of America looking at the WR and KR, let's shift our gaze to the Peashooter (above, opposite), another Dain G. favorite. I'll also confess that I get weak in the knees whenever I see an early-era Harley

flat track or board track racer. Those were
the bikes that formed the foundation for the
phrase "Harley Wrecking Crew," a term that
has been used to describe Harley-Davidson's
dominance on the dirt-packed racetracks of
America ever since, and a phrase I used often
in my race reports when I was Sport Editor
for *Cycle Guide*.

As we journey back in time, into the 'teens
and beyond, we finally come to the bike
that started this 100-plus-year movement—
Serial No. 1. I recall gazing at this bike when
it was on display at the Harley-Davidson
Museum in Milwaukee, Wisconsin, and

thinking that this was the acorn that led
to the mighty oak we know as the Harley-
Davidson Motor Company.

There you have it, some of my favorite
Harleys. I'm sure you have yours in mind,
too, so if we ever meet at a bike show or run,
I hope that you'll share with me the Harleys
that get your moto-juices flowing. In the
meantime, I hope that you enjoy reading
about the following 51 Harleys as much as I
enjoyed writing about them. Ride safely!

Dain Gingerelli
Mission Viejo, California

CHAPTER 1
A COMPANY DEFINED

Fittingly, the story of the Harley-Davidson Motor Company begins with a bike that has become known as Serial No. 1. Four young men—William Harley and brothers William, John, and Arthur Davidson—built the bike in 1903, basing their design on a rudimentary single-cylinder engine that they wedged into a loop frame that was an evolution from bicycle-frame designs of the era. Records are sketchy, but it's believed that the industrious Milwaukee boys built as many as eight similar bikes the following year. Regardless of the number, the fact remains that their hard work and entrepreneurial genius resulted in what eventually grew to become America's premier motorcycle company, surpassing all other brands in this country.

Through the years, the Motor Company has experienced hard times and good times, but one fact remains—the bikes that were produced during the company's formative years set the tone of the industry for the remainder of the twentieth century. The bikes in this section not only represent Harley-Davidson's formative years but also stand for the engineering and marketing prowess that made the company what it is today.

Heritage plays a key role among Harley owners for several reasons. Foremost, Harley-Davidson's hallowed history stretches back to 1903 with the origins of this bike, Serial No. 1. Four men—William Harley and the Davidson brothers, William, Walter, and Arthur—were responsible for the bike's genesis, and they are as much a part of the Motor Company's heritage as the bikes that made Milwaukee famous.

But every Harley rider will remind you "it's about the bikes," and with that, let's

SERIAL NO. 1
Price: NA
Horsepower: 3
Engine Displacement: 26.84 cubic inches
Engine Bore & Stroke: 3x3-1/2 inches
Weight: 180 pounds
Number Produced: 1

have a look at what Serial No. 1 has to offer. Its single-cylinder 26.84-cubic-inch engine has a bore and stroke of 3x3-½ inches,

and a series of rods and linkages connect the left-hand throttle to the rudimentary carburetor positioned behind the cylinder. Final drive is via a leather belt that transfers power to the 28-inch-diameter rear tire. A roller chain is part of the bike's starting system.

The 180-pound motorcycle's frame had no suspension other than the spring system that supports the solo seat. Remember, 1903 marked the early years of the fledging motorcycle industry, so designers were working essentially from a blank sheet of plans.

Did You Know?
The bike shown here is actually a 1905 chassis with internal engine parts bearing Serial No. 1. Its engine originally displaced 24.74 cubic inches, but was later bored to displace 26.84 cubic inches.

Chuck Yeager, who helped pioneer the world of flight beyond the sound barrier, once said that aviation progress was marked with "black holes in the earth." Applying Yeager's philosophy to the advancement of motorcycle technology, the 1909 Model 5-D could be considered one of the industry's black holes toward progress. This was Harley-Davidson's first V-twin engine to reach the assembly line and eventually the dealer's showroom floor. It was also a failure—a big, beautiful failure that helped Harley engineers and management gain invaluable insight for future models and for how the Motor Company would conduct business to maintain its reputation.

The engineers' lessons? Foremost, that the Model 5-D's intake valve design, based on the de Dion–Bouton system that relied on suction to open the intake valve, wasn't suitable for V-twin engines. There's also speculation that lack of a tensioner in the Model 5-D's belt drive created its own set

of problems that were later rectified for future designs.

Records show that the factory recalled all 27 Model 5-D bikes. And that was management's lesson—to confront a problem head on. The 1909 recall proved important two years later when Harley-Davidson introduced an improved iteration of the 45-degree V-twin engine, a model that not only is considered a landmark among enthusiasts today but was well received by customers back then.

1909 MODEL 5-D

Price: $325
Engine Displacement: 30 cubic inches
Engine Bore & Stroke: 3.3125x4 inches
Wheel Size (F/R): 26/26 inches
Number Produced: 27

Did You Know?

A V-twin displacing 49.98 cubic inches was introduced in 1909, but mechanical gremlins prompted Harley-Davidson to discontinue it. An improved V-twin was introduced in 1911.

1909 MODEL 5-D

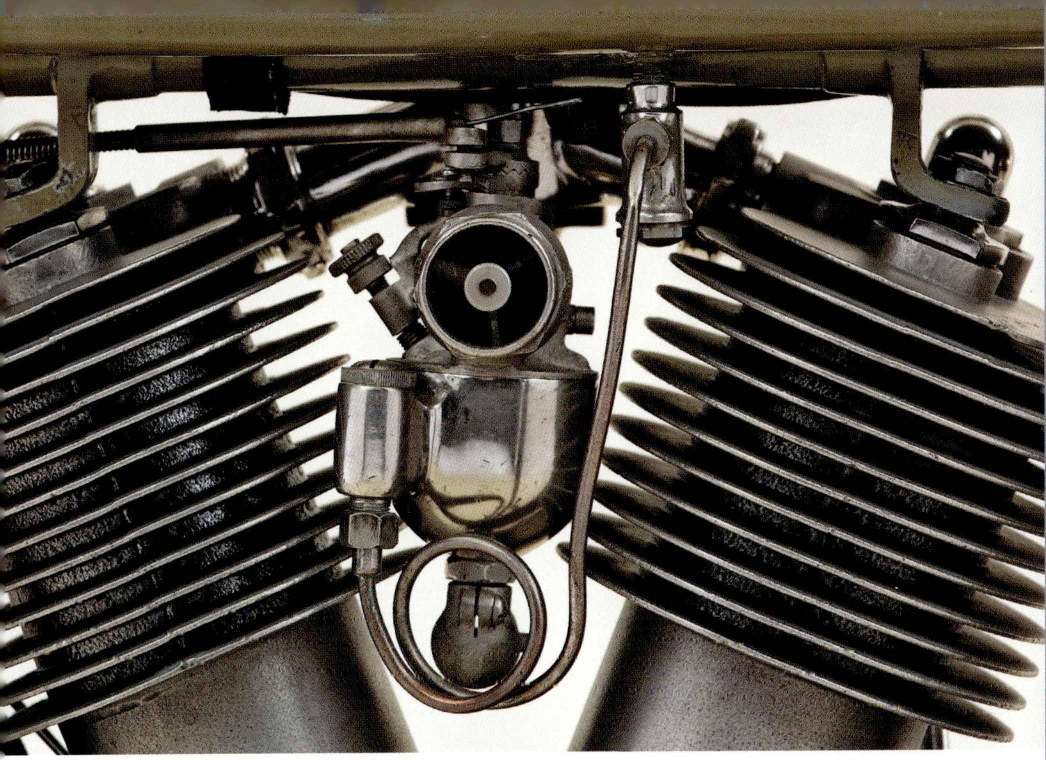

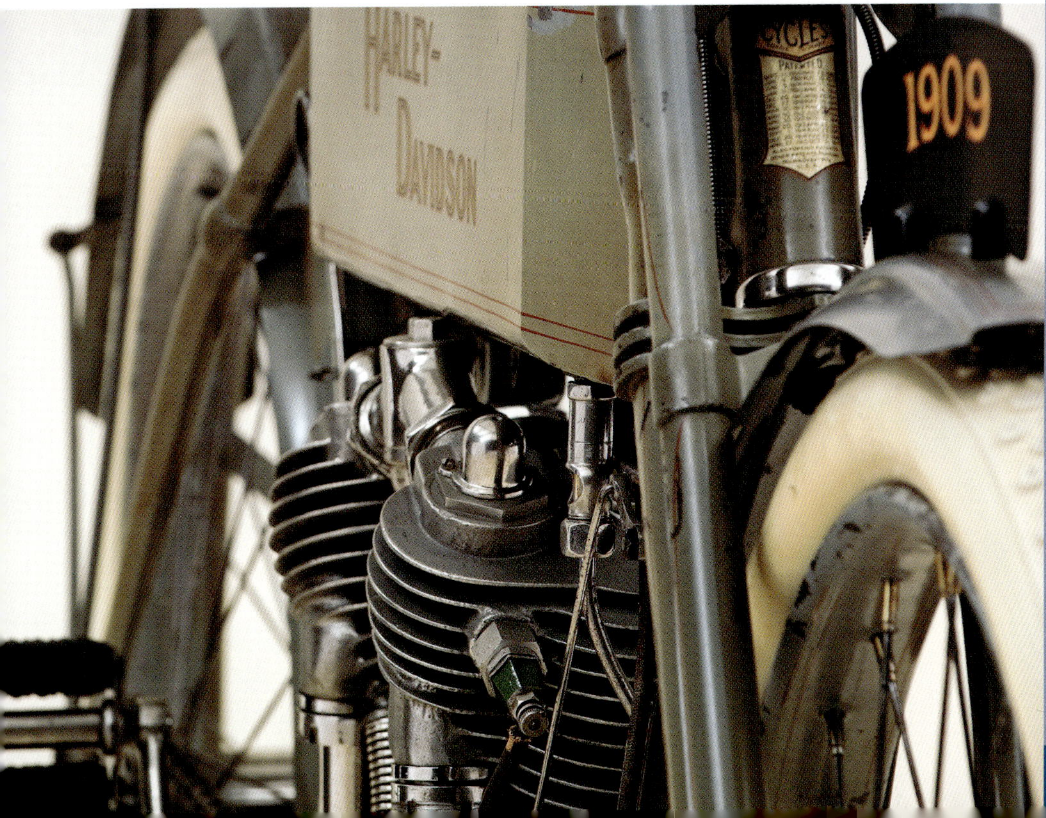

Look closely at the 1912 Model X-8-A and see if you can spot its most significant feature. Give up? Then check out the seat's placement on the frame. From 1903 through 1911, all Harleys used frames that were an evolution from bicycle frames, and so the seat was always perched atop a center post that positioned the rider rather high in the

1912 MODEL X-8-A

Price: $235
Engine Displacement: 30.16 cubic inches
Number Produced: NA

saddle. By placing a small bend at the rear of the frame's backbone, and changing the shape of the tank at the rear, the Model X-8-A's seat was positioned lower than on any Harley-Davidson built before. This positioning helped lower the bike's center of gravity for improved handling.

Moreover, a spring inside the new frame's vertical post beneath the seat helped cushion the ride. A pair of progressively wound coil springs externally placed under the seat made the ride softer yet. Harley-Davidson called the new system "Ful-Floteing Seat," and despite its unorthodox spelling, the arrangement worked. Enough so that by year's end 545 Model X-8-As were sold.

New technology was applied to the drivetrain as well, with a free-wheel control placed inside the rear wheel hub. The lever on the left side of the gas tank controls the clutch, so the rider doesn't need to pedal for acceleration. Modulating the clutch lever and throttle made for better, smoother starts.

Did You Know?

The 1912 V-twin engines were available in two displacements—the D measuring 49.48 cubic inches and the E at 60.34 cubic inches.

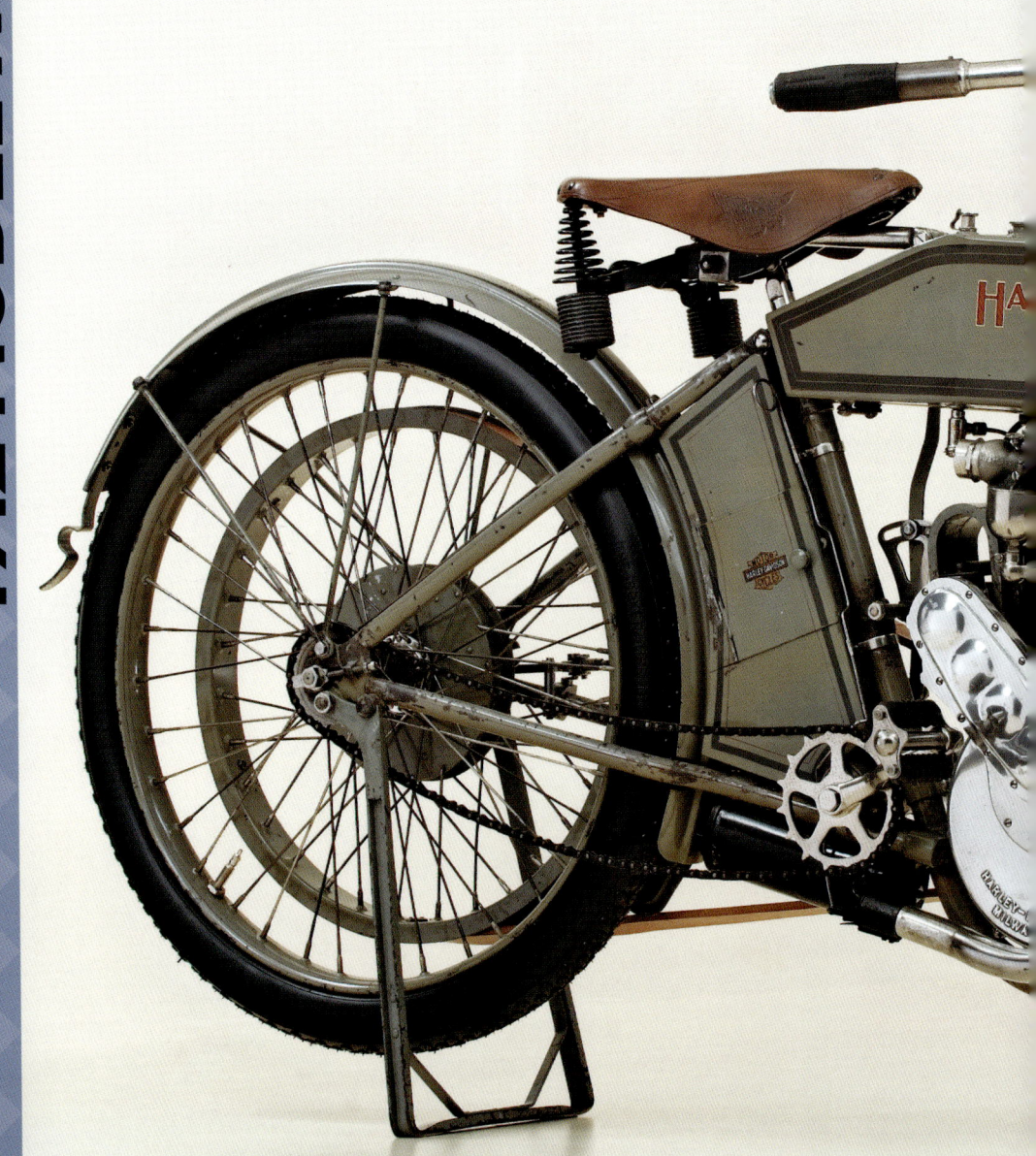

1912 on the number plate. "DSON" (HARLEY-DAVIDSON) visible on the tank.

The Model 9-E was the best-selling Harley-Davidson for 1913, with 6,732 units produced. That accounted for more sales than all other models (9-A, 9-B, 9-F, and 9-G) combined. Like the 1912 Model X-8-A, the 9-E was offered with Ful-Floteing Seat and the Free Wheel Control rear-hub clutch assembly. But while the 8-X-A used a single-cylinder engine, the 9-E was powered by a larger 60.34-cubic-inch V-twin.

1913 MODEL 9-E

Price: $350
Horsepower: 8
Engine Displacement: 60.34 cubic inches
Engine Bore & Stroke: 3.5000x3.3125 inches
Weight: 312 pounds
Wheelbase: 56.5 inches
Wheel Size (F/R): 28/28 inches
Top Speed: 68 miles per hour
Number Produced: 6,732

Indeed, the V-twin engine in Harley's lineup for 1913 was based on the same F-head design that debuted in 1911. Unlike the ill-fated V-twin that Harley tried in 1909, the new engine's intake valves were operated mechanically for more precise adjustments. The V-twin's displacement increased during this time, too, from the 1911's 50 cubic inches to 60.34 cubic inches for the 1913 9-E model. Horsepower jumped from 6.5 in 1911 to 8 in 1913—about a 20 percent gain!

These improvements didn't go unnoticed by motorcycle consumers, either. By 1913, many of the early motorcycle manufacturers had gone out of business, leaving only a handful to forge ahead as the world headed toward its first global conflict in 1914. And Harley-Davidson Motor Company was among the top three remaining brands in America.

Did You Know?

Despite stiff competition from Ford Motor Company in terms of price for the fabled Model T car, sales for Harley-Davidson motorcycles continued to climb in 1913.

With exception of the Model 10-A, leather belt final drives had been replaced on all Harley-Davidsons by more efficient roller chains by 1914. The Motor Company introduced an improved starting system as well. Called the Step-Starter, the new system allowed the rider to start the engine with the bike on or off its center stand. The rider could stand next to the bike and apply pressure to a single pedal to fire up the engine. The system was designed so that the mechanism would not kick back.

A new two-speed transmission located in the rear hub was offered on three of the five models available in 1914. The additional gear afforded a more flexible power delivery, and a foot-operated clutch lever assisted during gear changes.

Up to 1914, engines had their valvetrains exposed, but a new enclosure system around

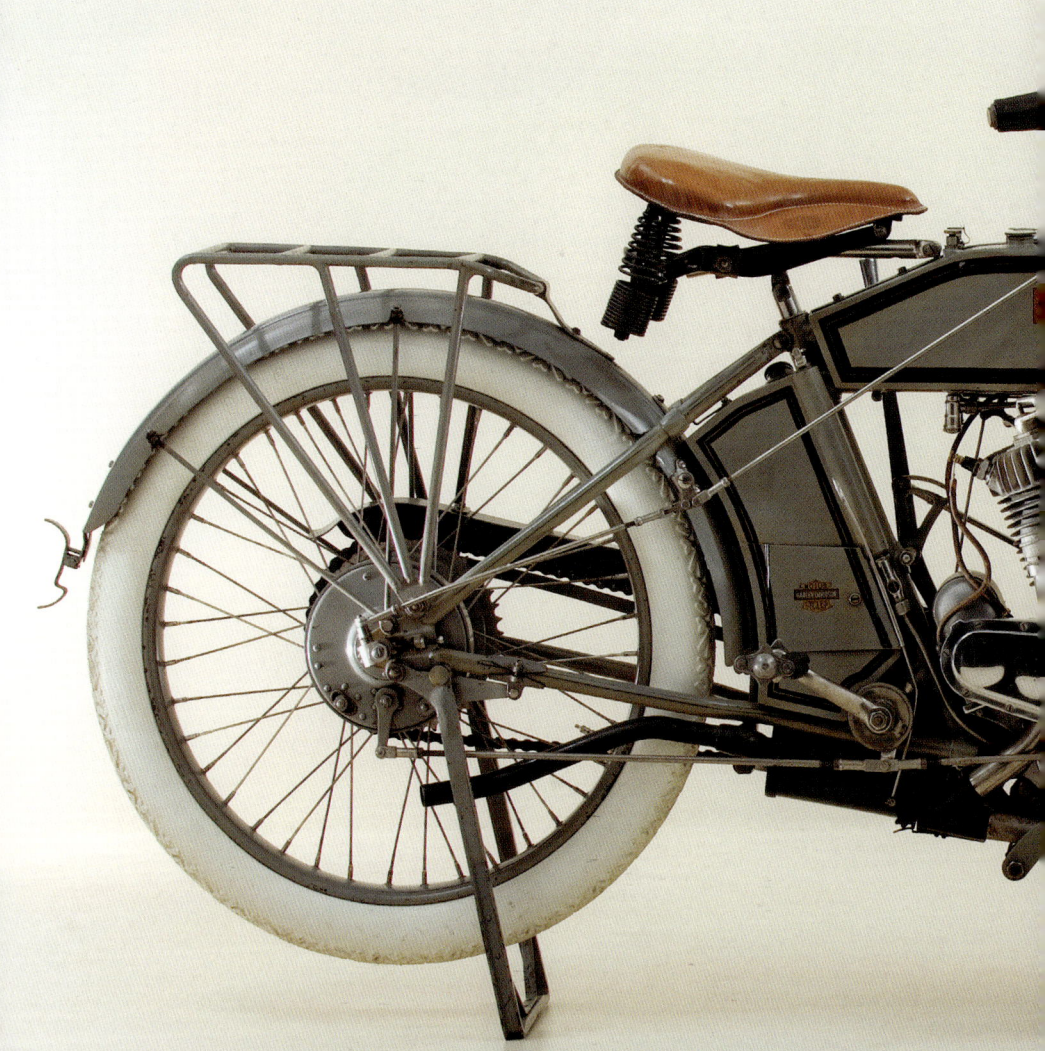

the coil springs helps shield the 10-F's top end from the elements. Similar technology was applied to the primary and final drive systems with guards to keep them enclosed. For rider comfort, footboards were mounted just ahead of the starter pedals, and for further safety and comfort, a brake pedal was added to the bike's right side. Records show that the 10-F was Harley's top-selling model in 1914, with 7,956 units built.

1914 MODEL 10-F

Price: $285
Engine Displacement: 60.34 cubic inches
Weight: 310 pounds
Wheelbase: 56.5 inches
Wheel Size (F/R): 28/28 inches
Top Speed: 65 miles per hour
Number Produced: 7,956

Did You Know?

Harley-Davidson developed its first official race-only motorcycle in 1914, and by the end of the year the Motor Company formed its first official factory team.

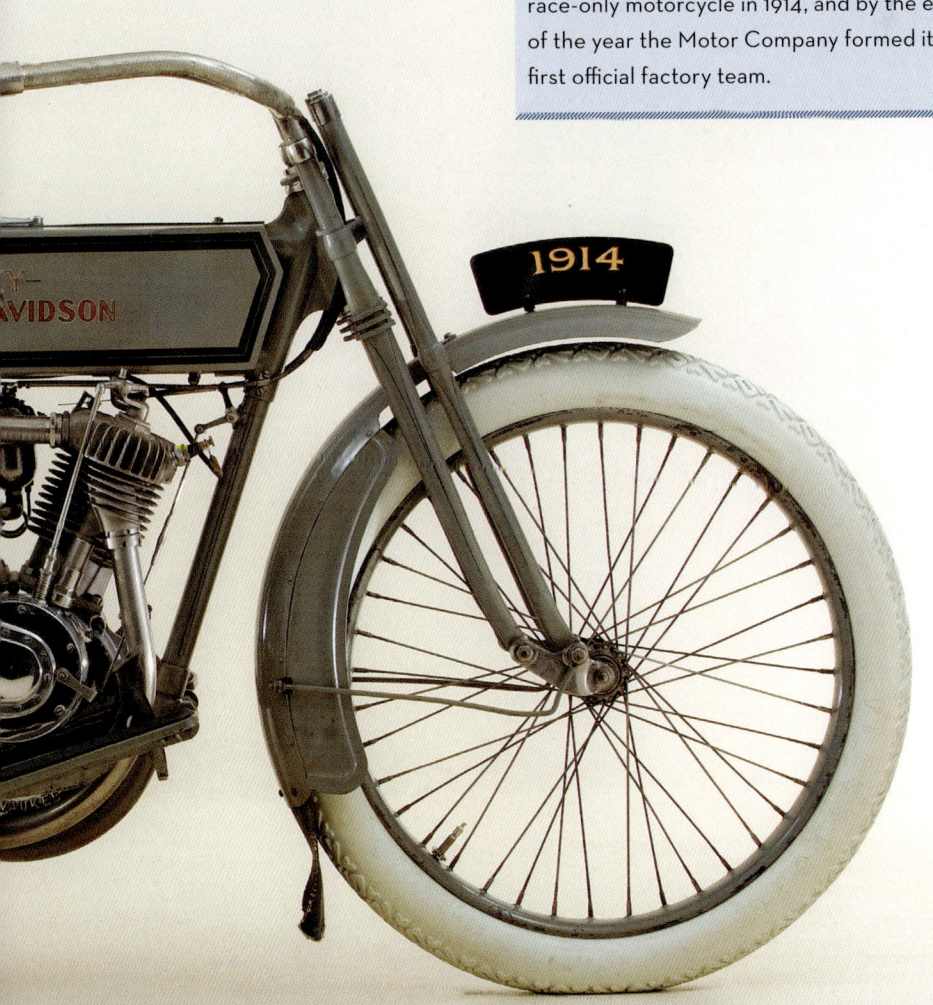

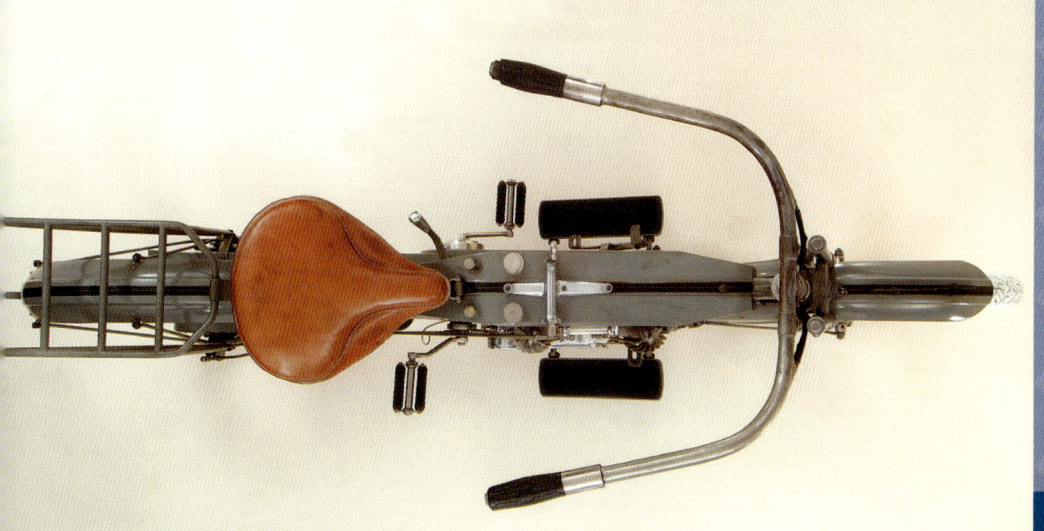

The concept that "bigger is better" worked its way into Harley vernacular for 1915. The bigger consisted of larger intake ports and valves for the V-twin engine, plus an improved Y-shape intake manifold. The better was more horsepower—about a 30 percent increase, from 8 to 11.

Reliability was factored into the improved engine as well. The connecting rods had roller bearings on their bottom ends, which also reduced friction within the engine's moving components. The engine also came with automatic oilers, another

first for Harley-Davidson. The gear-driven pump fed into the crankcase to assure that there was always a ready supply of lubrication for the engine.

But the story behind Harley's 1915 lineup, led by the 11-J, was about more than just the new engine and the horsepower it produced. Look closely at the 11-J featured here, and you'll see a three-speed transmission set behind its 45-degree V-twin engine. This marked the first year for the new box, considered a milestone in technology because it was

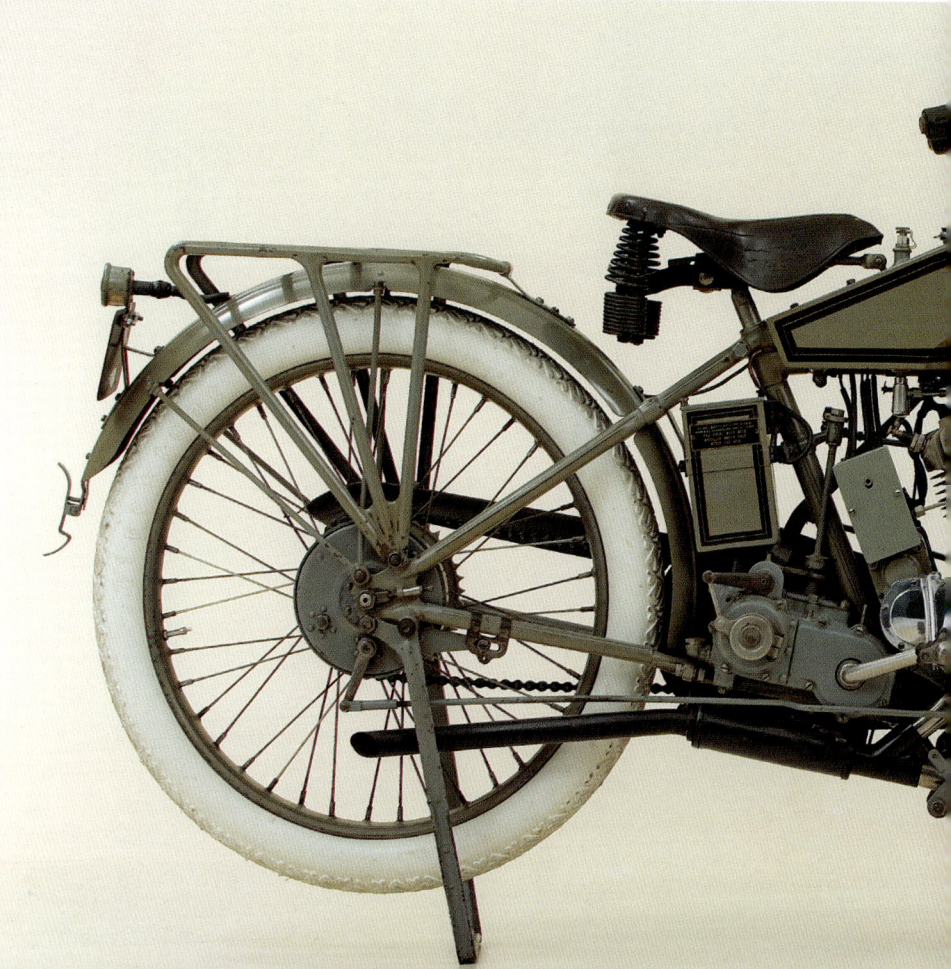

Harley's first transmission with more than two speeds.

The 11-J, along with the 11-H, was also the first Harley-Davidson available with electric lighting. Earlier models used lamps fueled with acetylene gas that was stored in small tanks on the bike. Electrical lighting was cleaner, more efficient, and broadcast a more direct beam ahead for the rider to see at night. Clearly, Harley-Davidson was helping lead the fledgling motorcycle industry out of its Dark Ages and into the heart of the twentieth century's Industrial Revolution.

1915 MODEL 11-J

Price: $310
Horsepower: 11
Engine Displacement: 60.34 cubic inches
Weight: 325 pounds
Wheelbase: 59.5 inches
Wheel Size (F/R): 28/28 inches
Top Speed: 60 miles per hour
Number Produced: 3,719

Did You Know?

Harley-Davidson sold 9,855 examples of the 1915 Model F, making it the company's all-time sales leader up to that point.

L 16502 K

As the Great War—eventually to become known as World War I—escalated in Europe, the industrial sector in this country began to lay plans for America's impending involvement. For its part, in 1917 Harley-Davidson instituted the new Harley-Davidson Quartermasters School (later renamed the Service School) to train military personnel in the maintenance and repair of the motorcycles that the U.S. Army had adapted for war use when General John J. Pershing's troops chased the Mexican revolutionary, Pancho Villa, in 1916. The

1919 MODEL 19-FUS ARMY
Price: NA
Engine Displacement: 60.34 cubic inches
Number Produced: 7,521

school is still used to train mechanics, although the curriculum is decidedly different today.

Whether it was by coincidence or by choice, Harley-Davidson also changed the basic color for its motorcycles in 1917, replacing the familiar gray with olive green.

Regardless, the military-like color remained the company's standard for civilian models another 16 years.

The Model 19-FUS Army, successor to the 1918 Model 18-FUS, represented the military version of the Model 19-F that was aimed at the civilian market. Both models continued use of the four-camshaft engine that debuted in 1917. The F-head, 60.34-cubic-inch, V-twin engine relied on a three-speed transmission to transfer power to the rear wheel. In addition, the worm gear–actuated clutch was replaced by a cam-actuated mechanism that proved to be more reliable. Combined production of the military FUS series from 1918 and 1919 was 15,616 bikes.

Did You Know?

Due to the war in Europe, most of Harley-Davidson's production of bikes for the U.S. military continued into early 1919. Only twin-cylinder models with three-speed transmissions were assembled for civilian use early in the year.

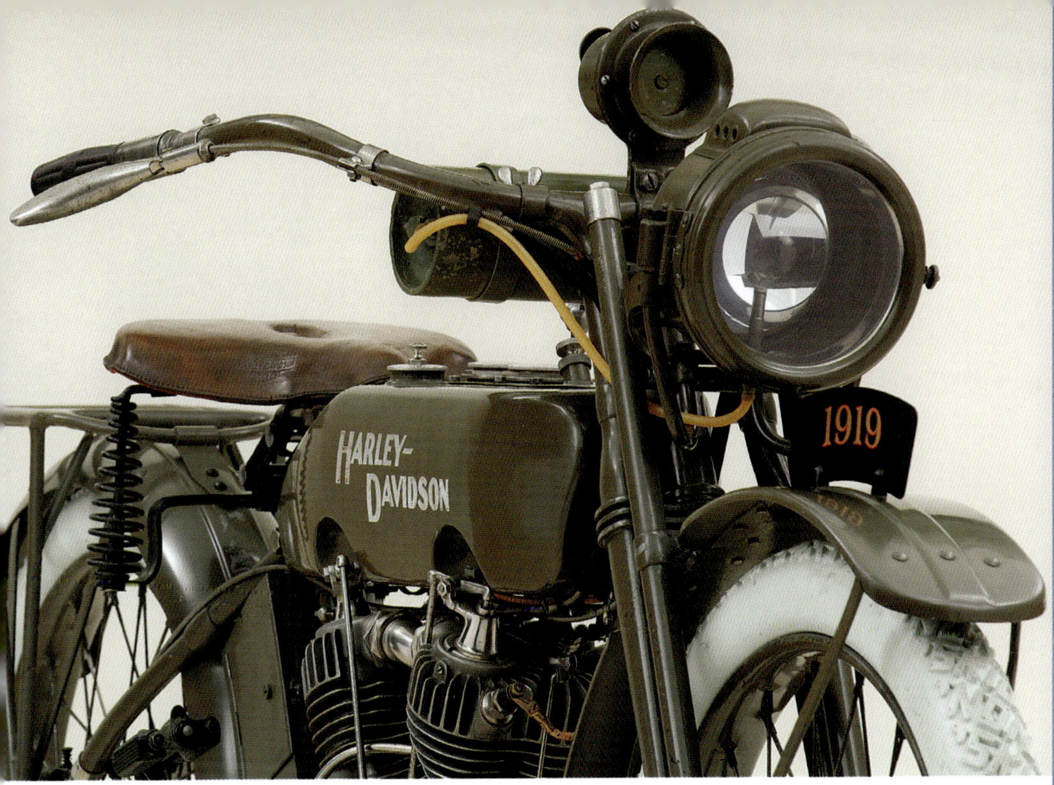
HARLEY-
DAVIDSON
1919

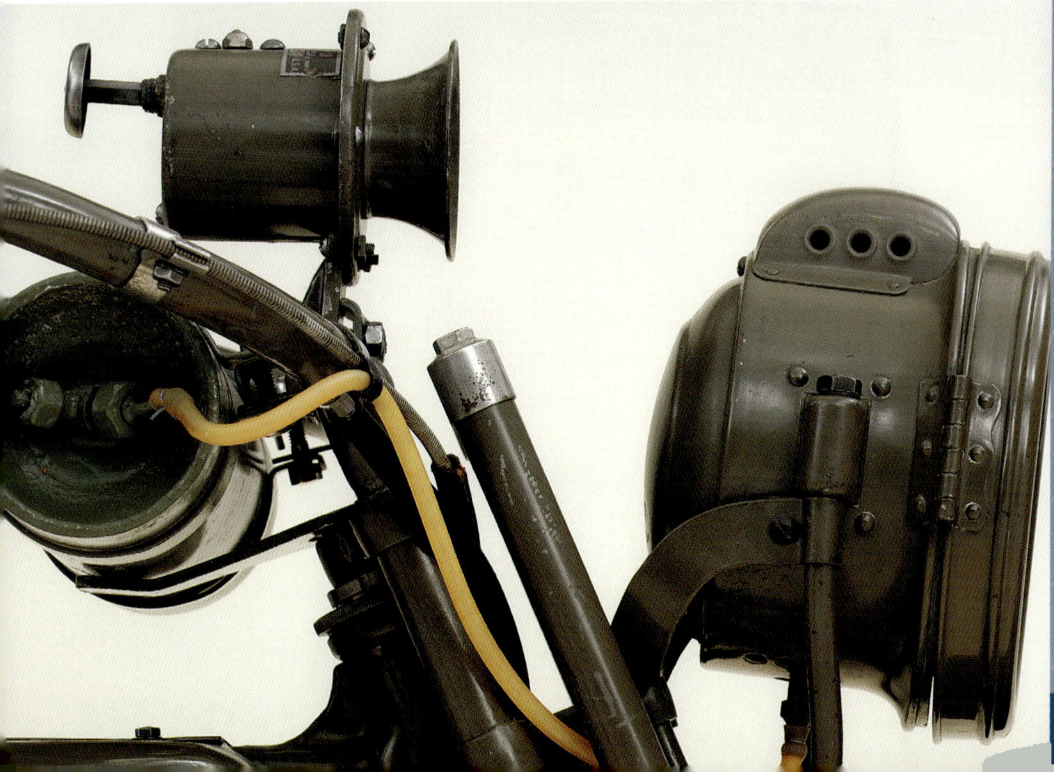

In a bid to attract entry-level riders, Harley-Davidson introduced the Model W Sport Twin in 1919. The engine was based on the design of the English-built Douglas that used a pair of opposed cylinders set longitudinally in the frame. The design allowed for a low center of gravity and, coupled with the bike's 257-pound weight, the Model W was considered to be a rather easy motorcycle to ride.

In addition, the low-slung engine incorporated features not found on

1920 MODEL 20-W SPORT TWIN

Price: $335
Horsepower: 6
Engine Displacement: 35.6 cubic inches
Weight: 257 pounds
Wheelbase: 57 inches
Wheel Size (F/R): 26/26 inches
Number Produced: 4,459

other Harley models. The three-speed transmission and clutch assembly were integral with the engine crankcase, and a stamped-steel case completely enclosed the drive chain to keep it clean. The engine's two cylinders displaced 36 cubic inches, enough to propel the Model W to a top speed of about 50 miles per hour.

Despite its user-friendly design, the Model W didn't sell well in America. Like today, American riders in 1920 seemed to prefer bikes powered by larger displacement engines, and so most of the 6,000 or so Model Ws made from 1919 through 1923 were sold to overseas markets.

A Model W ridden by Jack Fletcher as he and his bike ascended Southern California's 10,114-foot-high Mt. San Antonio was featured on the cover of the 1919 edition of *The Harley-Davidson Enthusiast*.

Did You Know?

The Model WF, introduced in 1919, was the first Harley-Davidson to receive a name along with its number-letter combination

1920

HARLEY-DAVIDSON

1920 MODEL 20-W SPORT TWIN

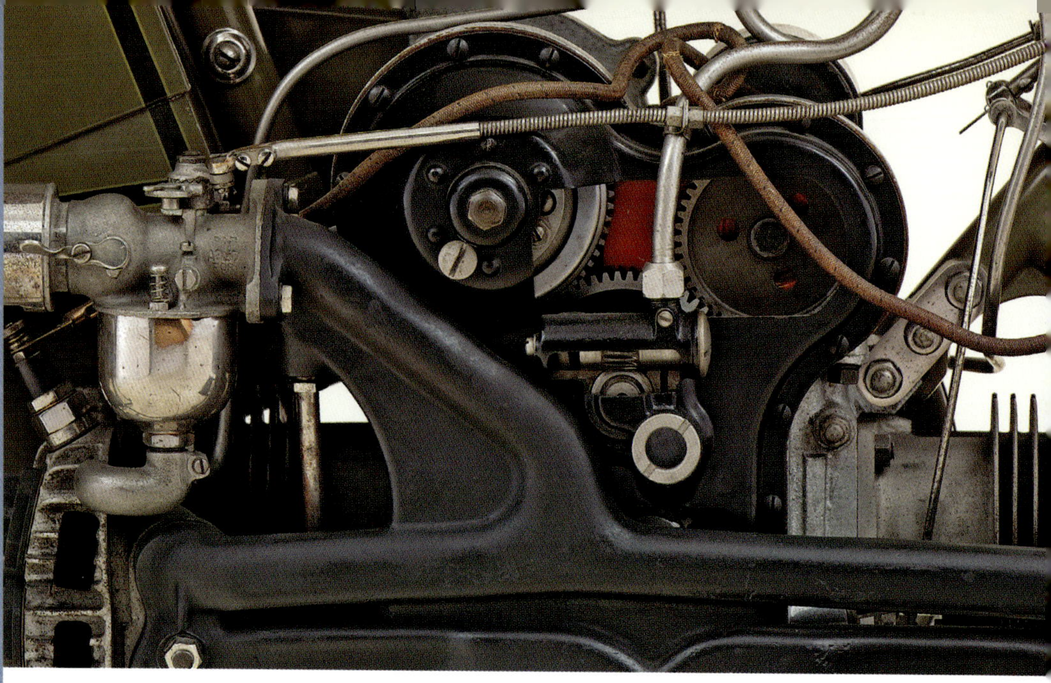

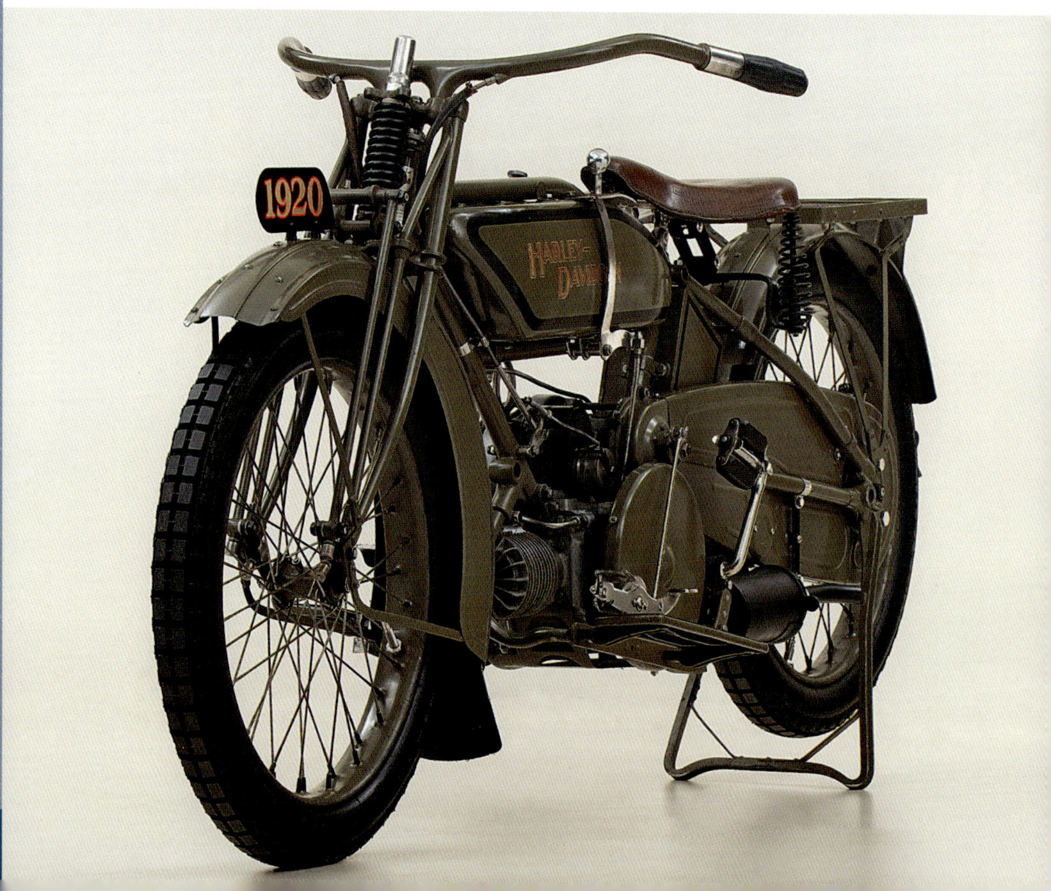
1920
HARLEY-

1920 MODEL 20-W SPORT TWIN

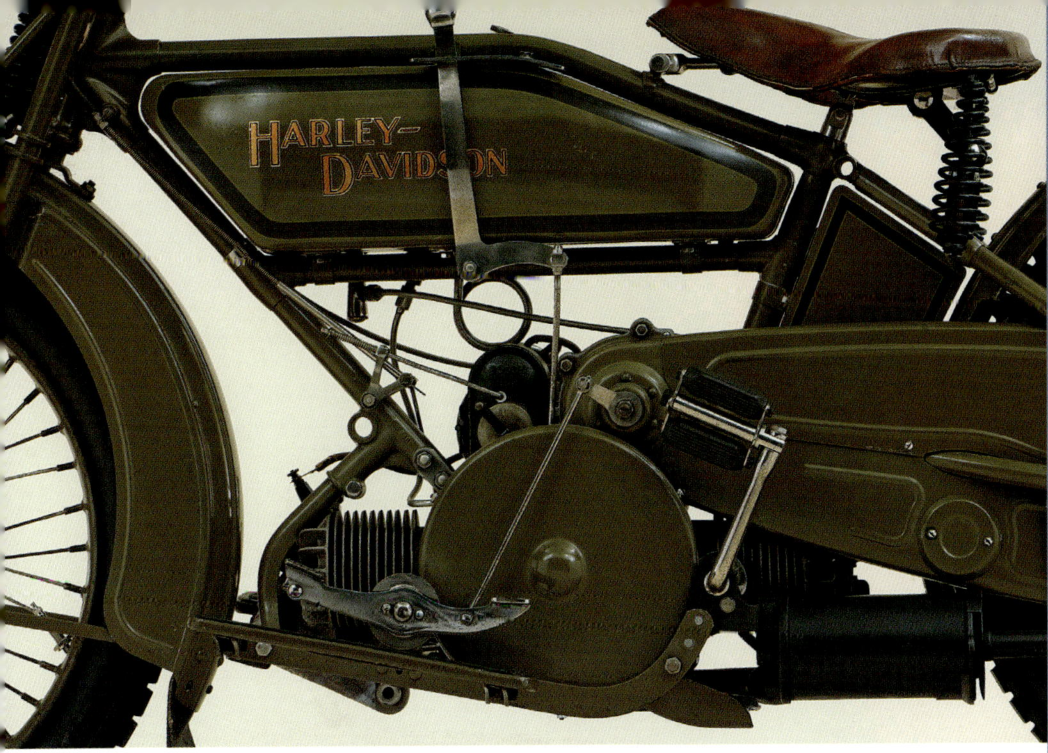

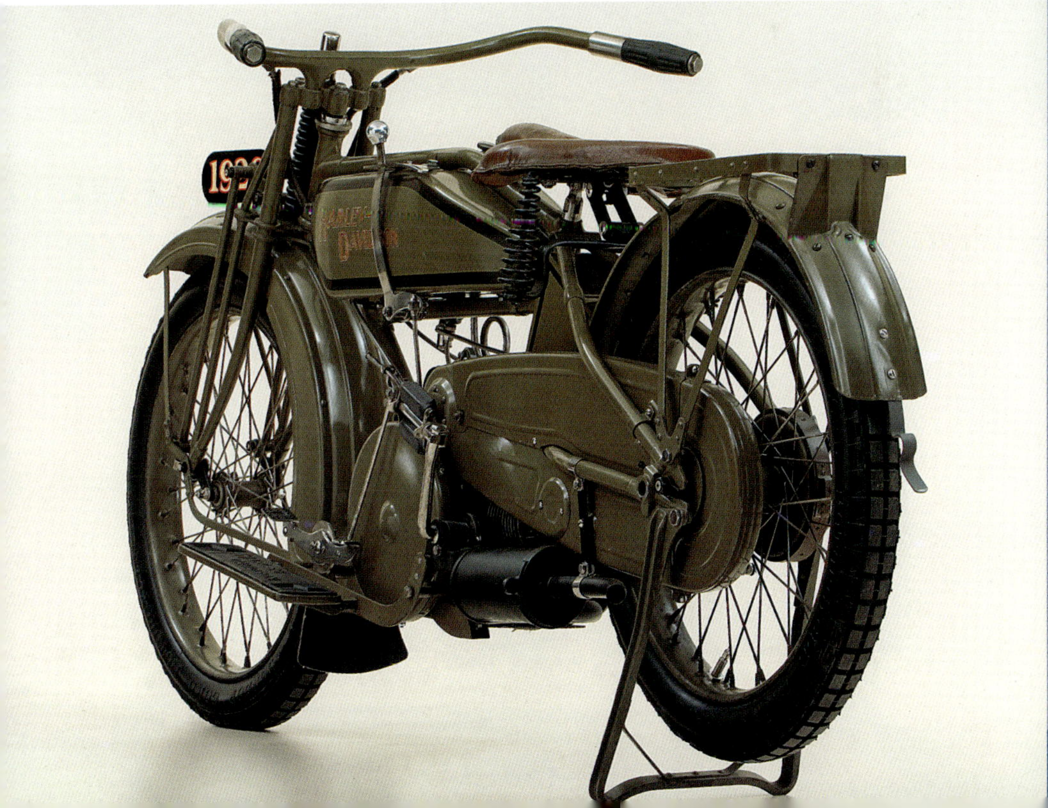

The 1921 model year saw some interesting additions to Harley-Davidson's lineup, perhaps chief among them the new 74-cubic-inch engine that joined the tried-and-tested 61-incher that had been in service since 1912. By 1925, it was time to update the big twin engines again, this time with a new frame listed in factory advertising as the Stream-Line. In all, 27 improvements were incorporated into the new frame, among

1925 MODEL JDCB

Price: $335
Horsepower: 24
Engine Displacement: 74 cubic inches
Engine Bore & Stroke: 3.44x4 inches
Weight: 405 pounds
Wheelbase: 59.5 inches
Wheel Size (F/R): 26/26 inches
Seat Height: Adjustable
Number Produced: 9,506

them a seat height that was 3 inches lower than before. Even so, the seat post cushion spring was increased in length from 9 to 14 inches for a softer ride. Additional frame rigidity was found in the front downtube, which was double butted and bolted to a steel channel serving as the base for the lower motor mounts.

Styling benefited, too, and 1925 models checked in with sleeker, more rounded

gas tanks. The wheel rims were wider to accommodate slightly larger tire sizes for improved handling, and the fork springs were improved for a softer ride as well.

Like all Harleys offered in 1925, the Model JDCB shown here has a three-speed transmission mounted behind its 74-cubic-inch engine. The JDCB has a fully charged electrical system; magneto ignitions were offered on some other models.

Did You Know?

All Harley-Davidson models in 1925, from the Model FE with its 61-cubic-inch engine to the 74-cubic-inch Model JDCB, were priced within $40 of one another.

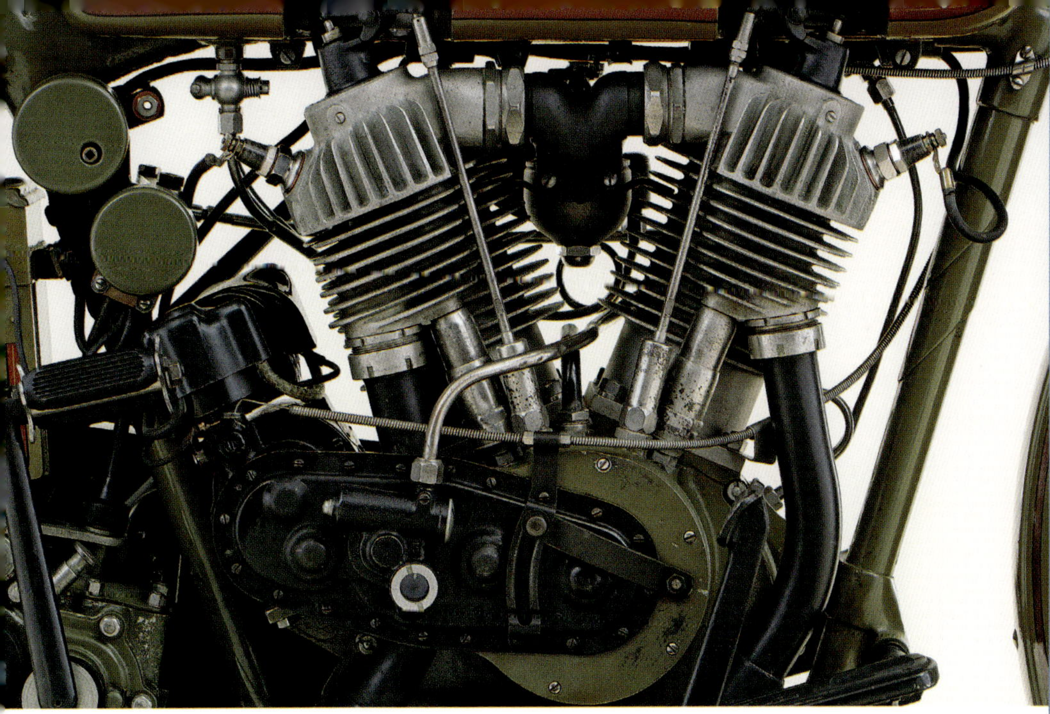

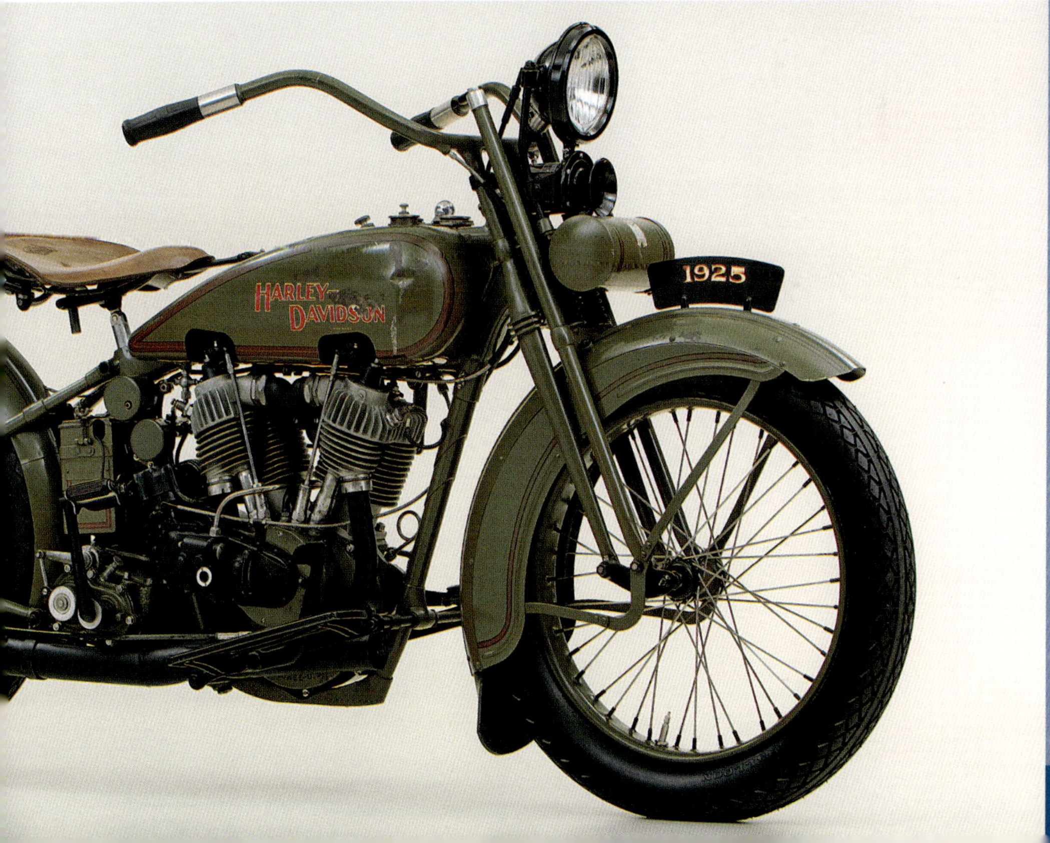

1925 MODEL JDCB

So you thought the twin-cam concept found on Harley-Davidson engines today is a recent innovation? Think again, because in 1928 Harley-Davidson introduced the Model JH, also known as the Two-Cam Sixty-One due to its 61-cubic-inch engine utilizing a pair of camshafts located in the engine cases to actuate the intake and exhaust valves. The new engine was a milder variation of Harley's race engine

1928 MODEL JH

Price: $320
Horsepower: 29
Engine Displacement: 74 cubic inches
Engine Bore & Stroke: 3.4x4 inches
Weight: 408 pounds
Wheelbase: 59.5 inches
Wheel Size (F/R): 18/18 inches
Top Speed: 85 miles per hour
Number Produced: NA

that had been so successful during the preceding years.

There were actually two displacement models available: the 61-cubic-inch JH and the 74-inch JD. Both used Harley-Davidson's by-then proven three-speed transmission. Standard color for all models was Olive Drab green, but various color options were available, among them the Police Blue with optional pinstripes shown here.

The following year, Harley-Davidson stylists gave the JH and JD twin headlights, a treatment most recently seen on today's Dyna Fat Bob. As you can see, while things change, they also remain the same!

Did You Know?

Harley-Davidson's first twin-cam engine was introduced in 1928, more than 70 years before the popular Twin Cam hit the market, first as the TC88 in 1999 and later as the TC96 in 2007.

1928 MODEL JH

1928 MODEL JH

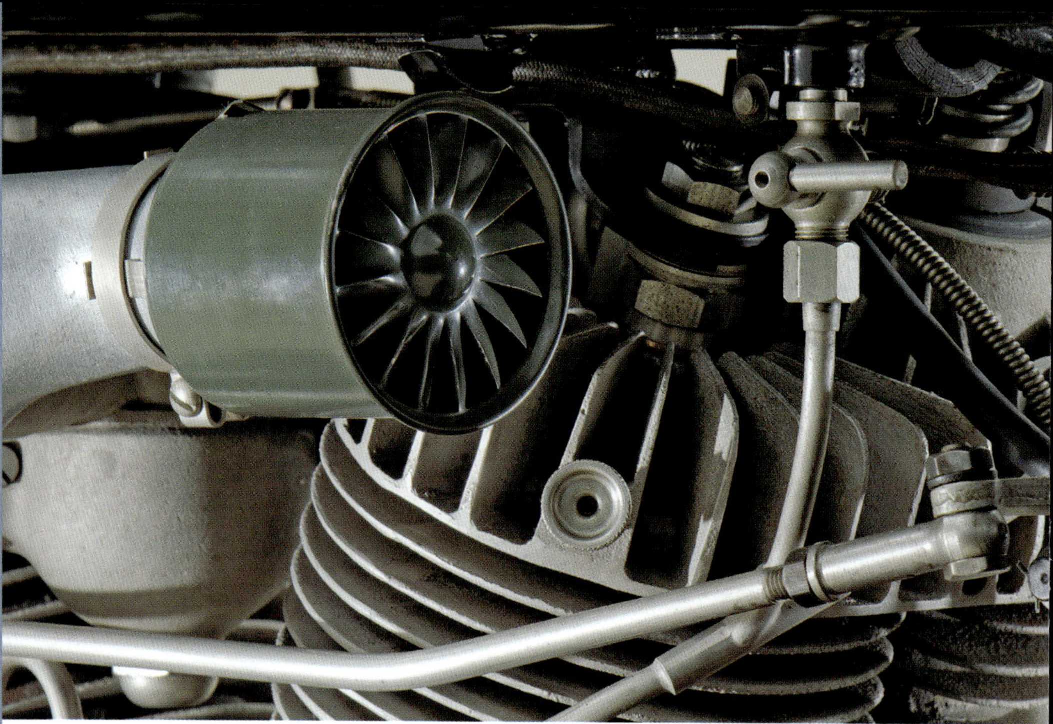

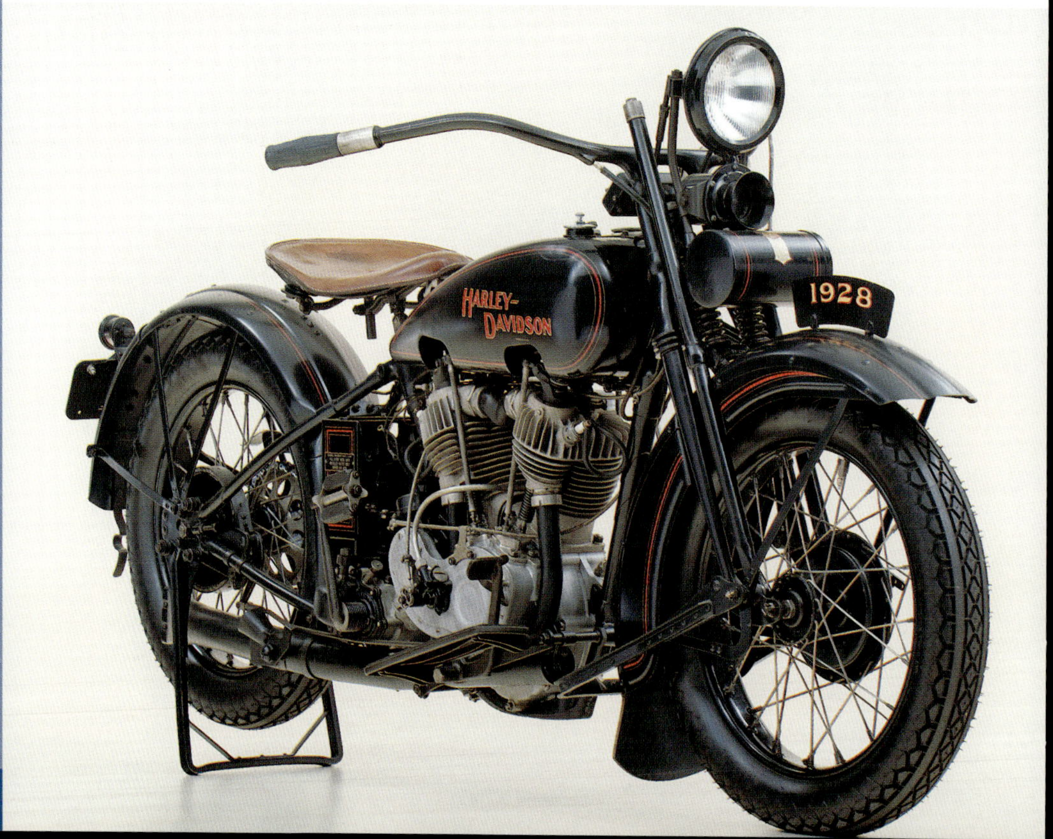

You might say that 1929 marked the beginning of a new era in what race historians term the Harley-Indian War. Prior to 1929, Harley-Davidson relied on its pocket-valve engine design to compete against Indian's Scout 101, which had a V-twin side-valve engine for power. The Scout was especially successful on the racetrack, dominating competition during the 1928 race season.

Harley's solution was to develop its own V-twin side-valver, which it did for model year 1929 when the D and DL bowed. This 45-cubic-inch engine was offered in two states of tune—the lower priced Model D had standard compression, while the DL had higher compression that translated to higher performance as well. The DL's compression ratio was rated at 5:1—low by today's standards, but in 1929 that was a rather

remarkable figure. The D's compression ratio was rated at 4.3:1. The new engine's bore and stroke measured 2.75x3.8 inches.

The compact Model D/DL used a single-downtube frame to cradle the engine, and 18-inch-diameter wheels and tires were set in a 57.5-inch wheelbase. Dry weight was 390 pounds, and suspension included a leading-link fork. For added rider comfort, the center post housed a coil spring for the seat.

1929 MODEL DL

Price: $290
Horsepower: 18.5
Engine Displacement: 45 cubic inches
Engine Bore & Stroke: 2.75x3.81 inches
Weight: 390 pounds
Wheelbase: 57.5 inches
Wheel Size (F/R): 18/18 inches
Top Speed: 70 miles per hour
Number Produced: 2,343

Did You Know?

The Model D was developed to challenge Indian's Scout 101. The D was rated at 15 horsepower, the DL's higher compression engine developed 18.5 horsepower, and the DLD produced 20 horsepower.

1929 MODEL DL

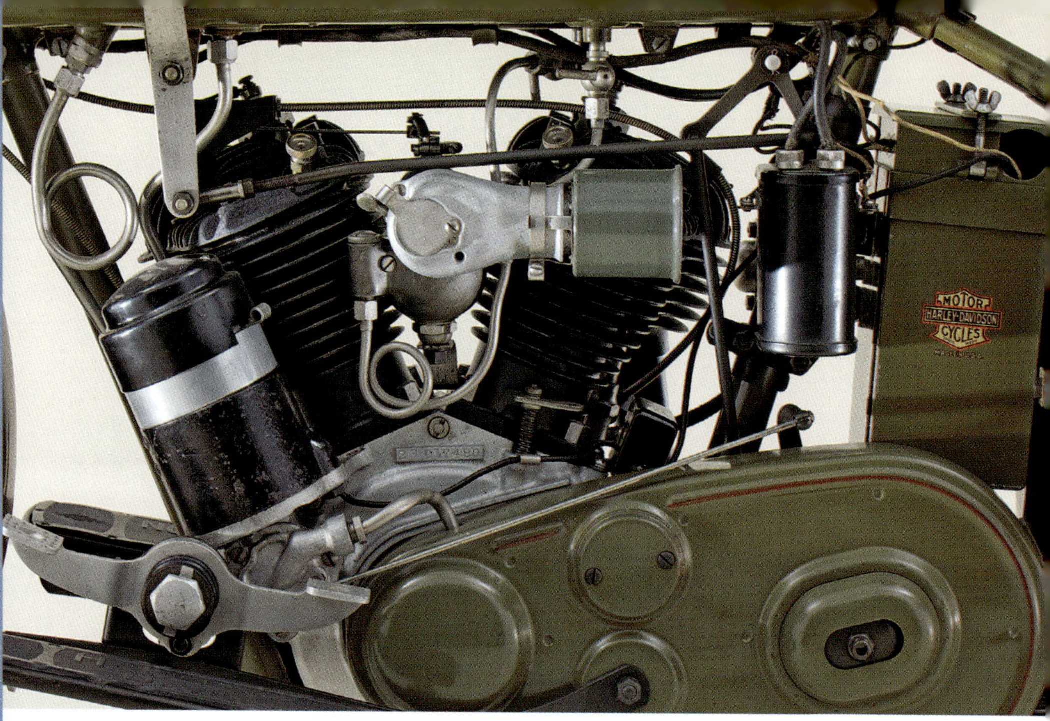

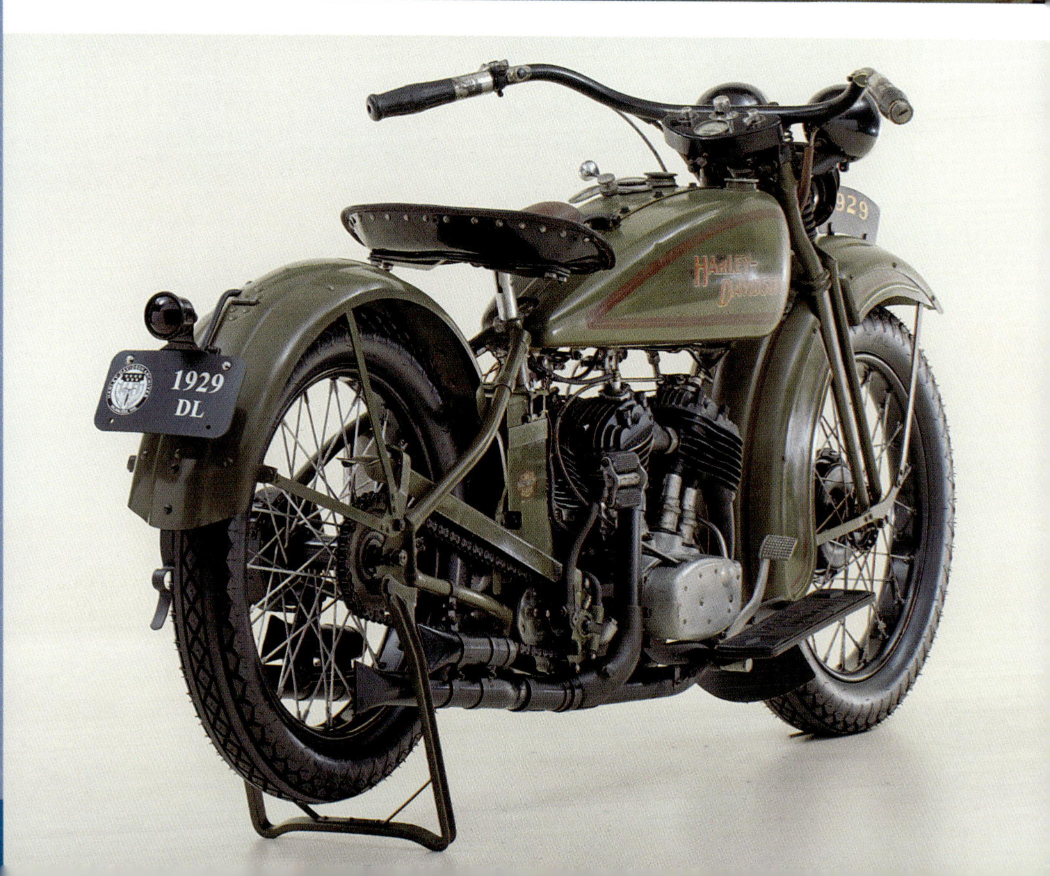

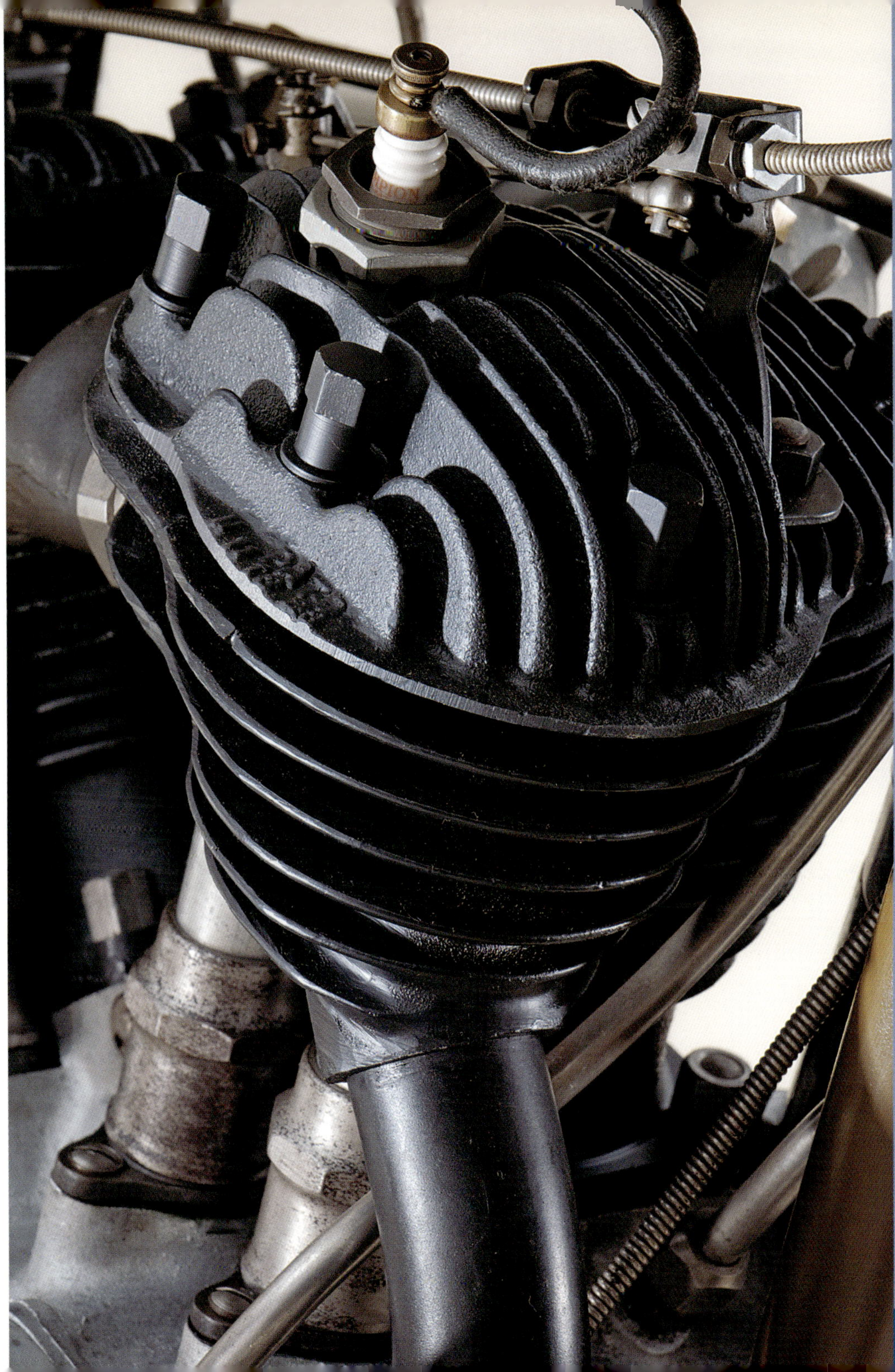

One of Harley-Davidson's most unique and longest running models debuted in 1932. That, of course, is the Servi-Car, a three-wheeler intended for commercial use by businesses looking to reduce costs for their transportation fleets. The Servi-Car is essentially half motorcycle and half, well, car. From the rider forward, the design is pretty standard fare for a conventional two-wheel motorcycle. The frame's steering head angle and length of the front fork are slightly different to maintain proper control while turning, but otherwise you're looking at half of a motorcycle.

Obviously, the Servi-Car's back half counters conventional motorcycle design. A pair of wheels and tires is found under a single body shell that includes a boxed compartment to store items inside and on top. The Servi-Car's most interesting feature, though, is its drivetrain. Like a car, the final drive includes a differential that helps compensate for wheel speed when making turns. Because the outer wheel must travel at a greater speed, a differential

1932 MODEL G SERVI-CAR

Price: $450
Horsepower: 22
Engine Displacement: 45 cubic inches
Weight: 598 pounds
Number Produced: NA

Did You Know?

Harley-Davidson marketed the Servi-Car as a time-saving vehicle for auto service establishments. Instead of sending two men off site to pick up a customer's car, a single mechanic could drive the Servi-Car to the customer and then hook up the three-wheeler to the customer's car and drive both back to the service station.

is spliced into the rear axle to distribute speed evenly between the inside and outside wheel while cornering.

The Servi-Car is powered by the 45-cubic-inch flathead engine introduced in 1928 for the 1929 model year. The three-wheeler remained in production from 1932 through 1973. In 2008, Harley-Davidson saw a need for another three-wheeler, resulting in the Tri Glide. Unlike its predecessor, the new trike isn't aimed at the commercial market but at riders looking to prolong their days in the saddle.

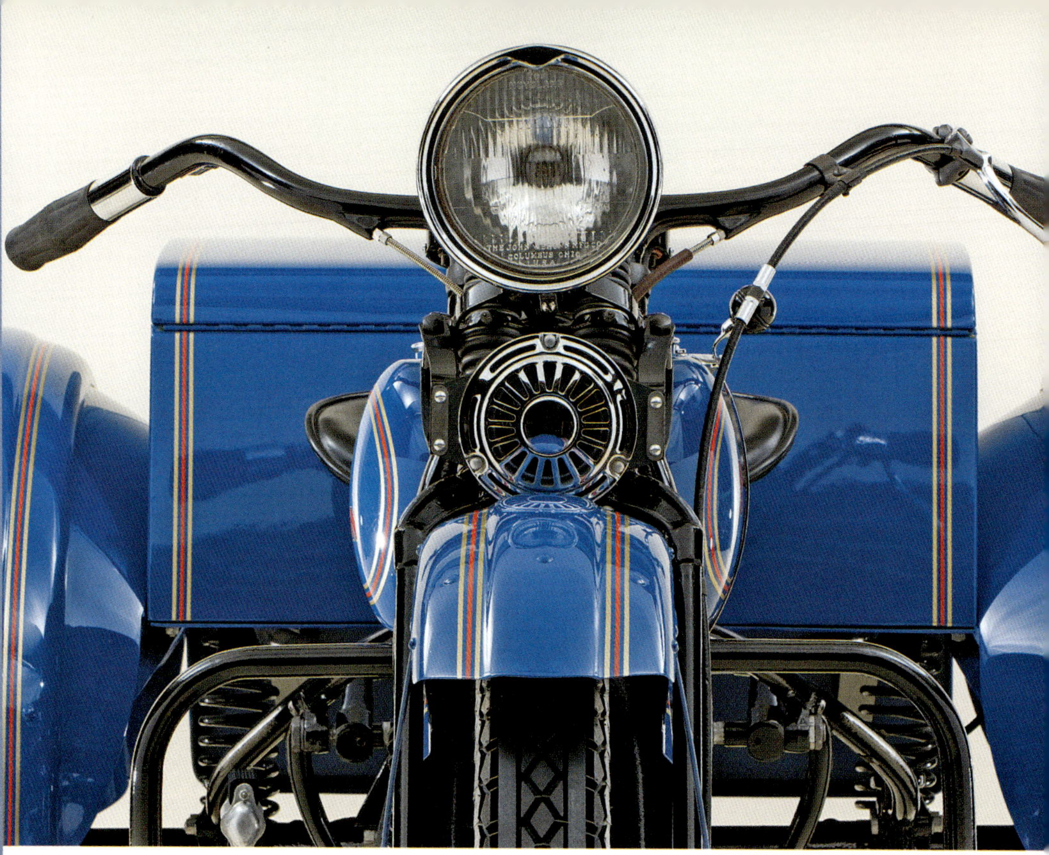

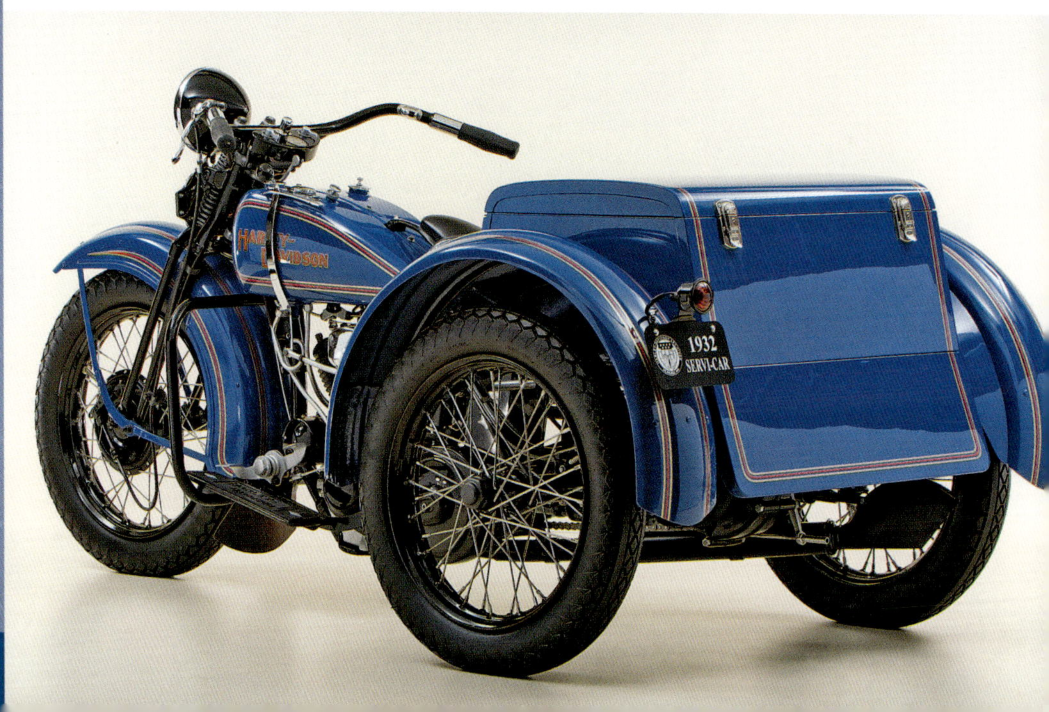
1932
SERVI-CAR

1932 MODEL G SERVI-CAR

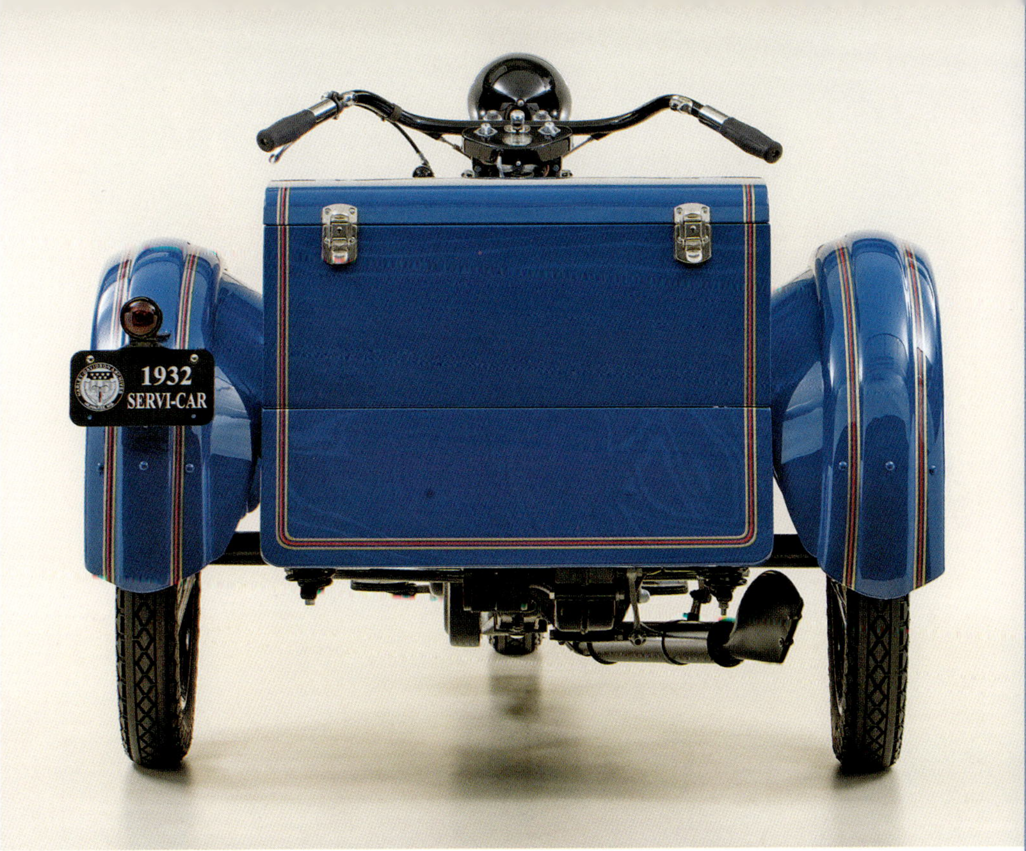

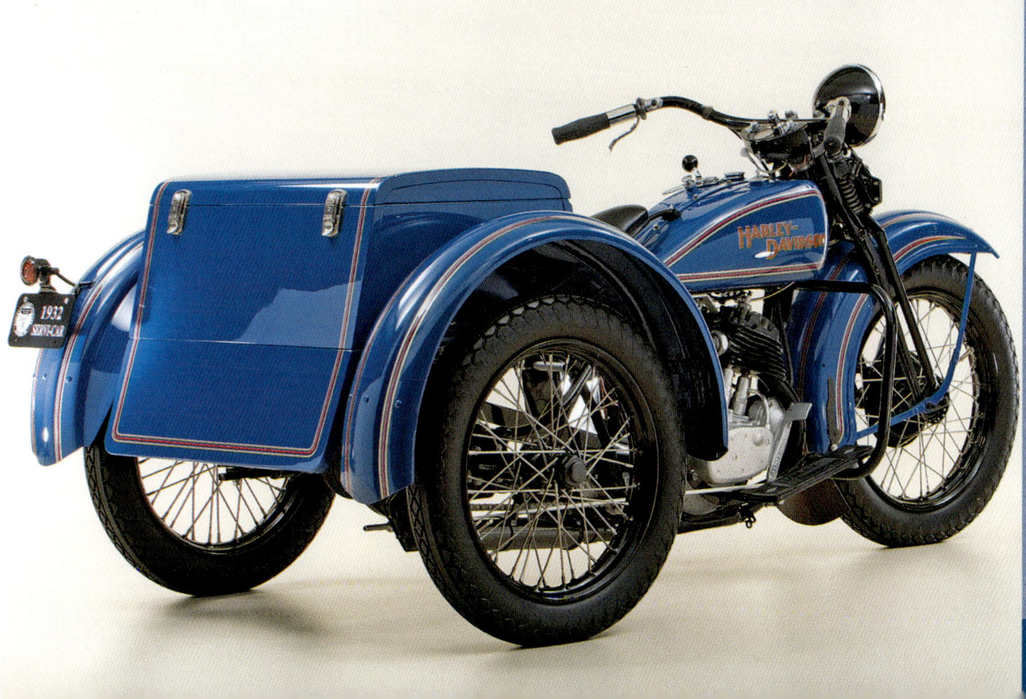

Harley-Davidson engineers hit on a successful formula in 1933, when they launched the Model VLD with what was marketed as the T.N.T. motor, because its new Y-shaped intake manifold and magnesium-alloy pistons helped increase horsepower by 20 percent over the standard VL 74-cubic-inch engine. The performance gain netted the VLD engine a claimed 36 horsepower, an impressive figure in 1933.

So how do you improve on a winning formula? First, you make it better with aluminum-alloy pistons that, while slightly heavier, are more reliable than their magnesium-based counterparts. You

1934 MODEL VLD

Price: $320
Horsepower: 36
Engine Displacement: 74 cubic inches
Weight: 390 pounds
Top Speed: 65 miles per hour
Number Produced: 780

also strengthen the frame and fork with a new heat-treating process, and finally you hand the entire package over to the styling department where the hot rod of Harley's fleet is given all new sheet metal.

And what a styling success this bike is! The valance fenders complement the curvaceous gas tank, and the theme is highlighted with Art Deco graphics and color schemes. Look further back and you'll see the latest Airflow taillight, and nobody can argue the uniqueness of the flip-up tailpipe.

The world economy was at an all-time low in 1934—the Great Depression was in full swing—but Harley-Davidson managed to sell 4,527 VLDs, far and above more than any other model in the lineup. The VLD is proof that if you build what the customer wants, they'll buy it!

Did You Know?

In 1933, a Model VLE (the engine with the highest compression ratio among the VL series) set an American speed record for production bikes of 104 miles per hour.

1934 MODEL VLD

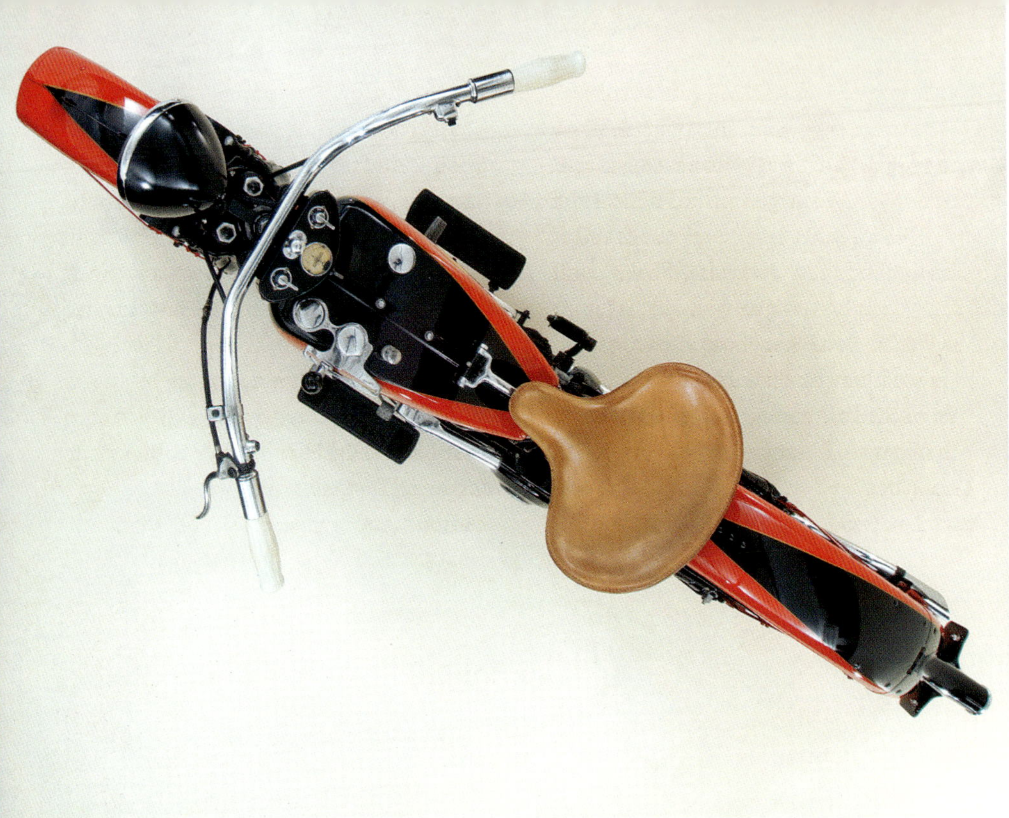

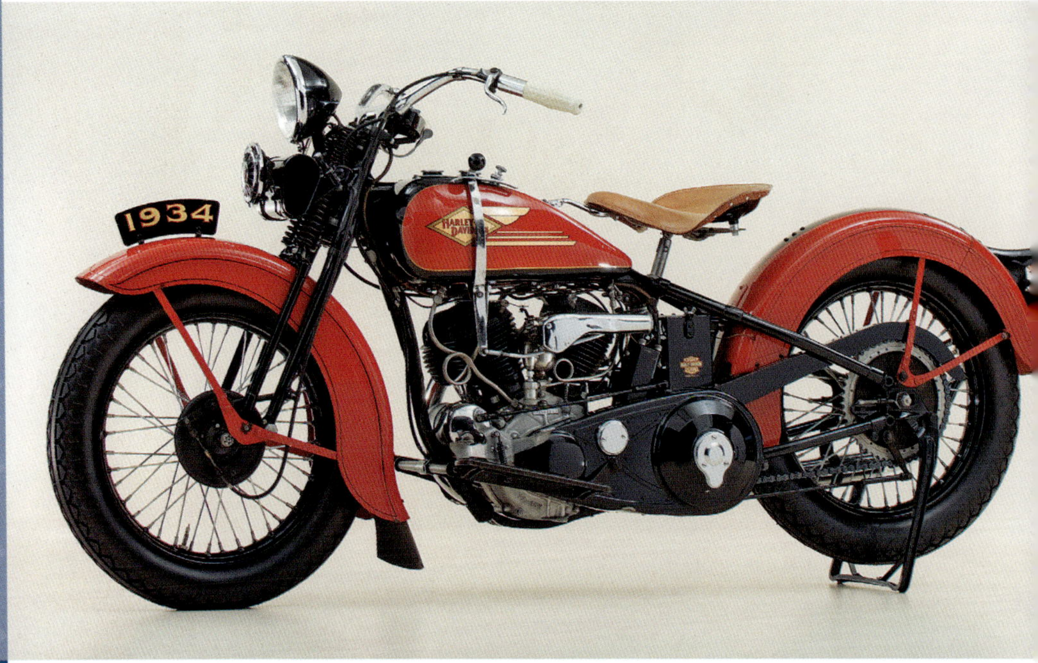

OIL
SECOND
HARLEY-DAVIDSON

ON
ON
PARK
ON
PARK
ON
AMPERES
5
0
5
10
10
DISCHARGE
CHARGE
MOTOR
HARLEY-DAVIDSON
CYCLES

1934
VLD

The big news in 1936 was the new Model E 61-cubic-inch overhead-valve engine that one day would become known as the Knucklehead. But when it came to supplying police departments across the country with motorcycles, Harley-Davidson stuck with a proven formula, and for 1936 that was the 80-cubic-inch VLH flathead (although some Model E police bikes were offered in 1936).

But Harley-Davidson did more than just supply the motorcycle to the respective

1936 VLH POLICE SOLO

Price: $340
Engine Displacement: 80 cubic inches
Wheel Size (F/R): 18/18 inches
Number Produced: 2,046

police departments. The Motor Company offered bikes as turnkey units that were ready to ride and chase the bad guys. The bike featured here includes the Deluxe

Police Group package that boasted the following ensemble: 100-mile-per-hour speedometer, receive-only radio with antenna and speaker, foot-operated siren, first-aid kit, rear fender rack, pursuit lights, and rack-mounted billy club, fire extinguisher, and flashlight. This bike had an optional windshield with stamped steel leg covers, too, and the bikes were painted in traditional police vehicle colors, usually at no extra charge.

Despite the VLH's service record, 1936 was the final year for this model. It was replaced in 1937 with an improved version of the flathead motor, and with the update came a new designation, the Model U.

Did You Know?

During the 1930s, some police departments used motorcycles to dispatch officers quickly to a traffic situation. The assigned officer was known as a Minuteman. When a traffic problem arose, the Minuteman was dispatched aboard his motorcycle to the scene.

1936 VLH POLICE SOLO

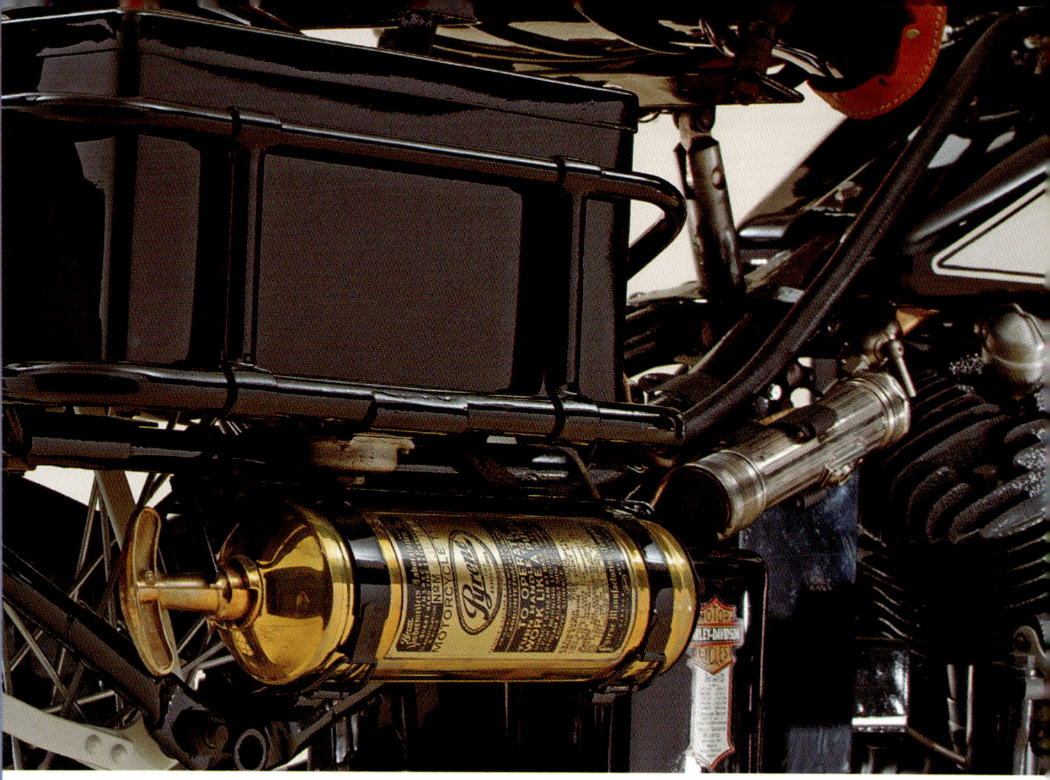

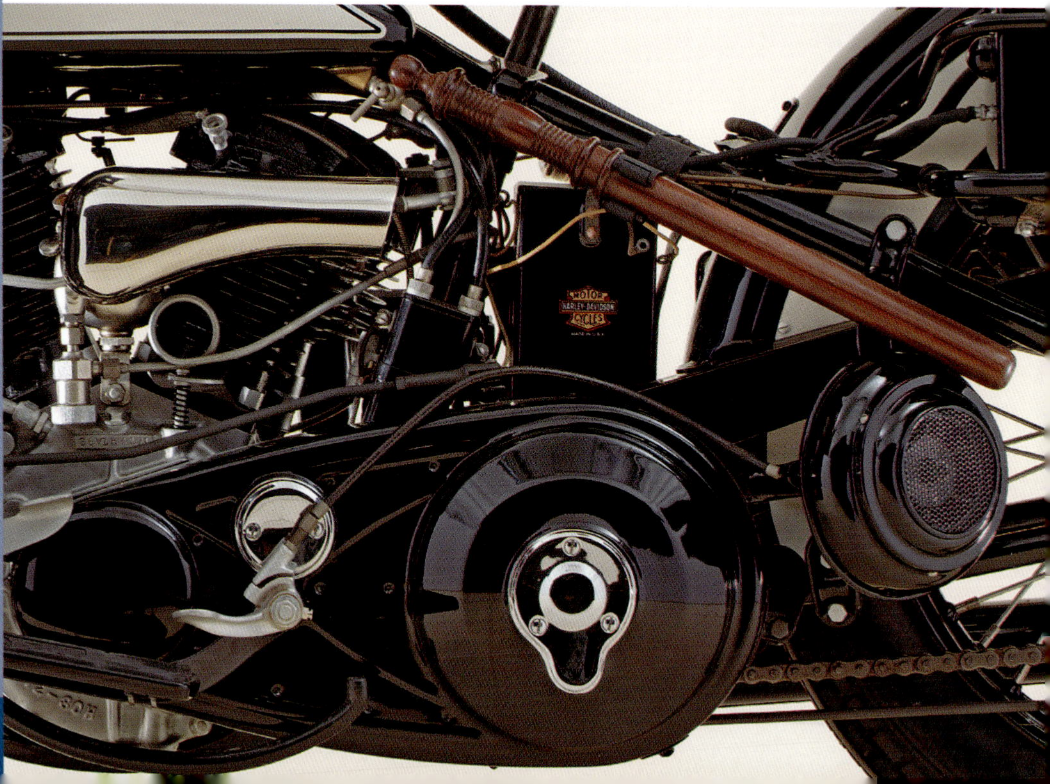

CHAPTER 2
KINGS OF THE HIGHWAY

If there's a definitive year that marks the beginning of the modern motorcycle era, it's 1936, for that was when the Harley-Davidson Motor Company revealed its new overhead-valve Big Twin to the world. At that moment, the motorcycle landscape changed forever. The F-head (inlet over exhaust) and L-head (flathead) engine designs were suddenly relegated to back room status. Harley's new 61-cubic-inch Model E, with intake and exhaust valves planted atop the combustion chamber, offered more power through a more efficient design.

But the Model E wasn't the only reason for the maturing of America's motorcycle industry during this time. When the United States entered the war against Germany, Japan, and Italy in 1941, Harley-Davidson, like all companies that composed America's industrial might, was called upon to support the war effort. Harley-Davidson engineers and workers answered the call, too, producing motorcycles in mass quantities for the Allied armed forces. In the process, they also developed some unique, even unorthodox, designs that were intended for one major goal—to defeat the Axis powers.

In this section, you'll read about some of those interesting military models that rolled out of Milwaukee for the war. History shows that we won the war, and you can bet that Harley-Davidson motorcycles played a key role in that victory.

Perhaps Harley-Davidson's most iconic model—other than Serial No. 1—is the 1936 Model E. For the E (and EL, which had higher compression) was the first Harley-Davidson V-twin to use an overhead-valve engine, making it the granddaddy of all Big Twin Harleys on the road today. And even though many of the E's technological features are no longer used, its DNA is found in all Big Twins built since 1936.

Previous Harley V-twin engines were based on the F-head (inlet over exhaust) or L-head (flathead) concepts. The E's overhead valves were set within a semi-hemispherical combustion chamber that produced a more efficient flame front. The result, in terms of performance, was 40 horsepower at 4,800 rpm for the EL. Impressive figures for the time.

Like all previous V-twins built by the Motor Company, the new air-cooled engine's cylinders were set at 45 degrees. But those jugs had a near square bore-and-stroke ratio of 0.946:1; bore was

3-5/16 inches and stroke was 3 1/2 inches for displacement of 61 cubic inches. Compression ratio was set at 6.5:1 (E) and 7:1 (EL), significantly higher than what either the F- or L-head designs offered previously.

Early E engines had exposed rocker arms and springs, but by year's end rocker covers were integrated into the design. The new covers resembled knuckles on a closed fist, which led to the engine's nickname of Knucklehead years later.

1936 MODEL EL

Price: $380
Horsepower: 40
Engine Displacement: 61 cubic inches
Engine Bore & Stroke: 3-5/16x3-1/2 inches
Weight: 515 pounds
Wheel Size (F/R): 18/18 inches
Top Speed: 100 miles per hour
Number Produced: 1,526

Did You Know?

The EL engine didn't earn its Knucklehead moniker until after an updated version of the iconic overhead-valve engine appeared in 1948. The new engine eventually earned the nickname Panhead. Only then did enthusiasts refer to the original OHV model of 1936–1947 as the Knucklehead.

1936 MODEL EL

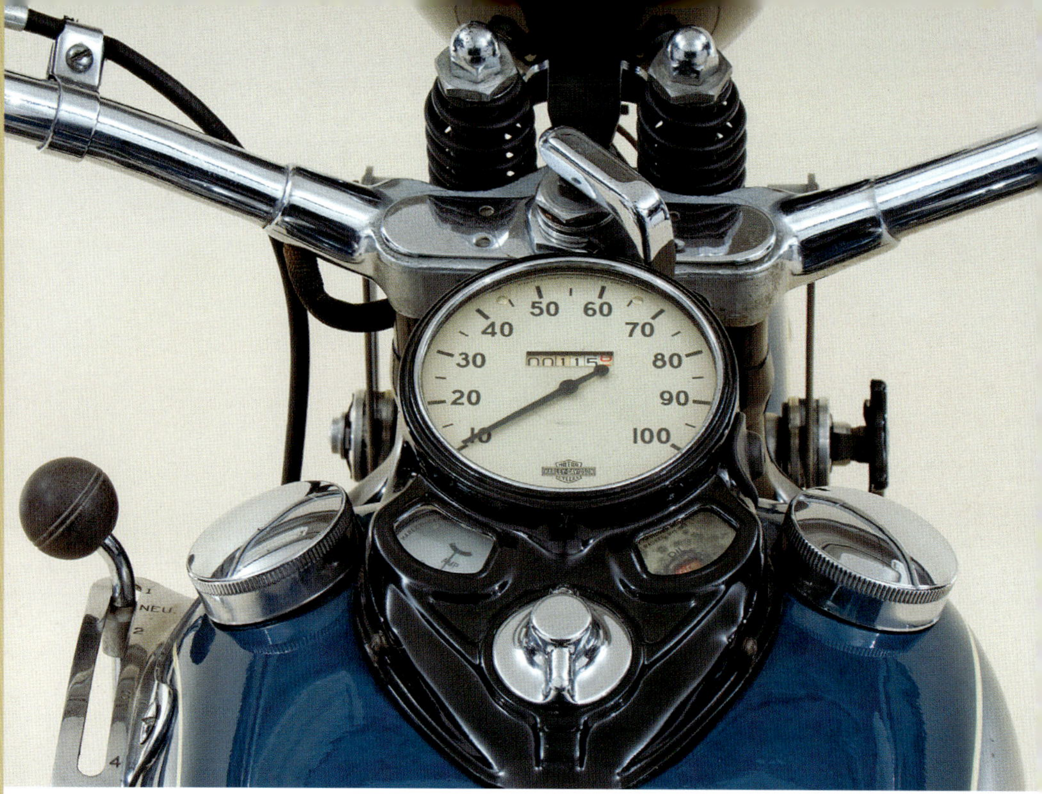

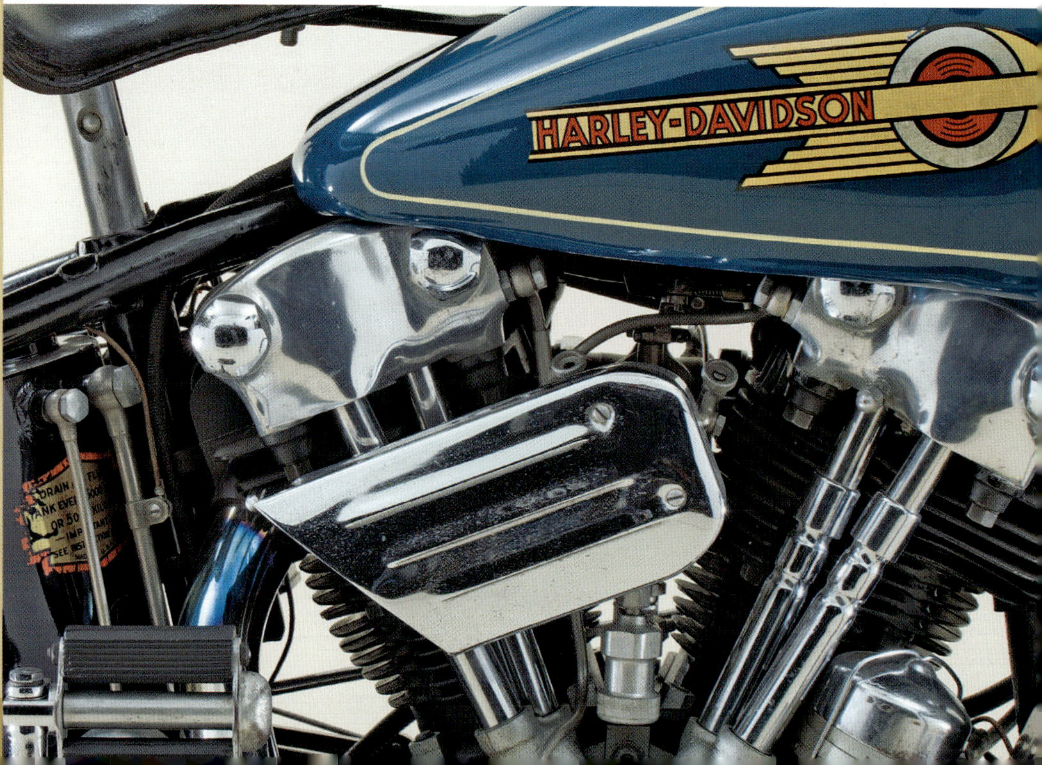

By 1939, the Servi-Car was a mainstay in Harley-Davidson's line of vehicles. Indeed, 15 models, ranging from the Model 39WL (retail $355) to the Model 39GDT Servi-Car ($530), were offered. This Model 39G was purchased by John A. Stanton for his Plymouth-Dodge automotive dealership in New York. The trike retains its original Teak Red and black paint with advertising logos and script that Stanton's shop applied.

The 1939 Servi-Car checked in with a few improvements over earlier designs. Foremost, the 1939 Servi-Cars were given larger storage boxes. The gain was two-fold, because the tow bar was now permanently affixed to the chassis rather than having to be stored inside the box. Tombstone taillights were placed on each rear fender (previous Servi-Cars had only one taillight) and, like all 1939 Harleys, the new cat-eye instrument panel was set atop the gas tank.

1939 MODEL G SERVI-CAR

Price: $515
Horsepower: 22
Engine Displacement: 45 cubic inches
Engine Bore & Stroke: 2.75x3.81 inches
Weight: 1,360 pounds
Wheelbase: 61 inches
Wheel Size: (F/R) 18/18 inches
Top Speed: 50 miles per hour
Number Produced: 320

Servi-Cars have always been a novelty among the automotive and motorcycle communities, and it's interesting to read what has been written about the design. One British motorcycle magazine described the three-wheeler as "The motor cycling equivalent of a pick-up . . . ." Showing a bit of cheeky British humor, that same magazine went on to state: "The 45ci (750cc) V-twin side-valver became a favourite with police departments. In town it was just the ticket for dealing with traffic and enforcing parking restrictions."

By 1937, the winds of war were again blowing over Europe, and fear in this country was that America would eventually be drawn into such a conflict. As a precaution and to prepare for such a calamity, the U.S. War Department invited Harley-Davidson, Indian, and Delco Corporation to submit motorcycles for testing for use in the armed services. The U.S. government stipulated that the bikes must be capable of fording streams and attain a top speed of 65 miles per hour.

Harley-Davidson submitted a variation of its WL, which ultimately became the

favored model. By 1945, more than 60,000 WLAs were built for the war effort. The military model of Harley's venerable WL, with its 45-cubic-inch engine, had a few modifications to ready it for combat duty. Chief among the changes was a slightly longer fork for increased ground clearance. A skid plate was placed underneath to protect against rocks and such, the headlight was mounted low to protect it during a crash, and a heavy-duty rear-fender cargo rack doubled as a place to mount two large leather saddlebags. A rifle scabbard was attached to the fork, and the fenders were placed high so that mud was less apt to build up between the tires and the sheet metal. The engine's compression ratio was kept at a mild 5:1 so it could burn practically any grade of gasoline while in the field.

1942 MODEL WLA

Price: $379.84
Horsepower: 23
Engine Displacement: 45 cubic inches
Weight: 576 pounds
Wheelbase: 57.5 inches
Wheel Size (F/R): 18/18 inches
Top Speed: 65 miles per hour
Number Produced: 13,051

Did You Know?
The WLA was based on the civilian WL, which sold for $380. That meant that the government got a 16-cent discount for each bike.

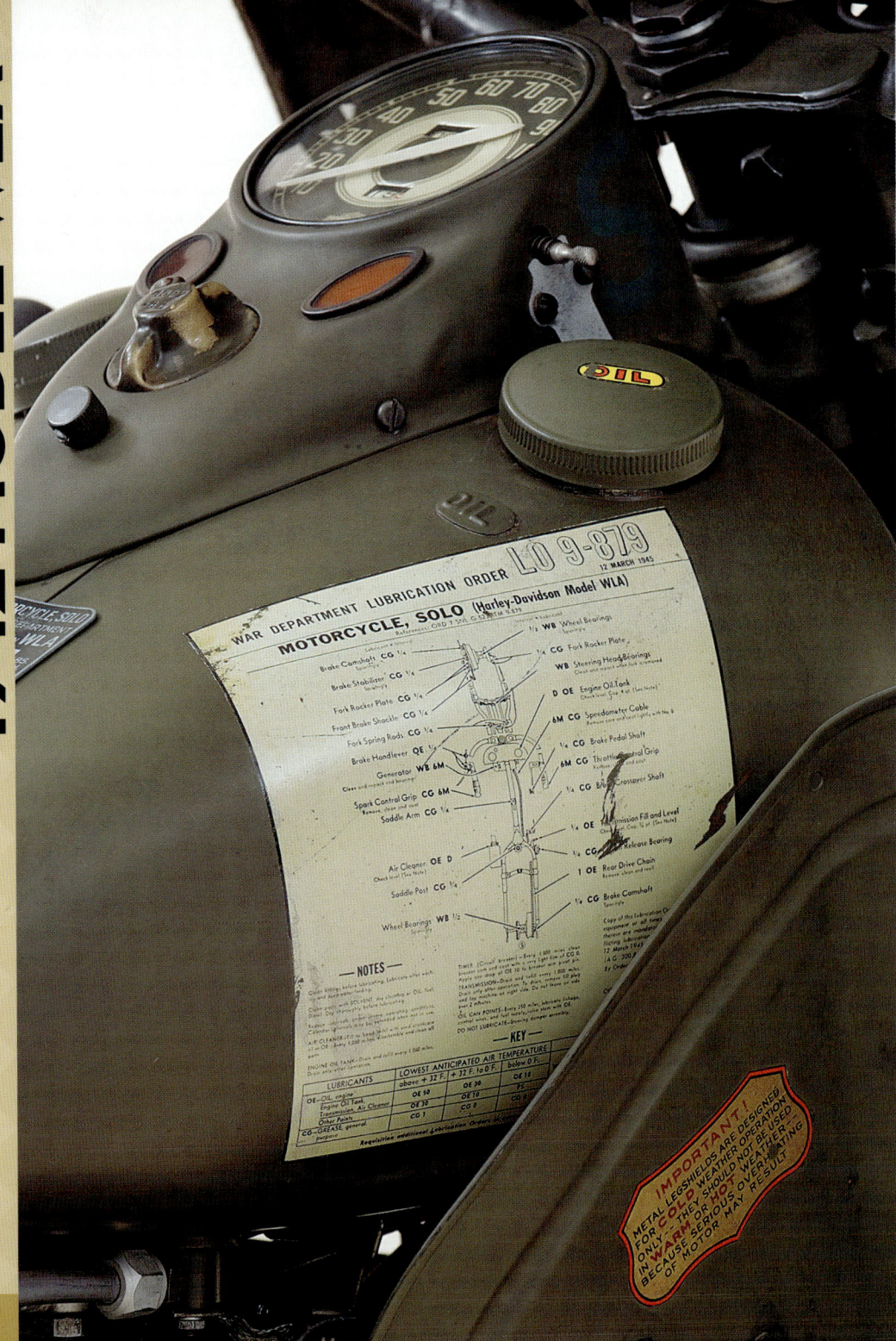

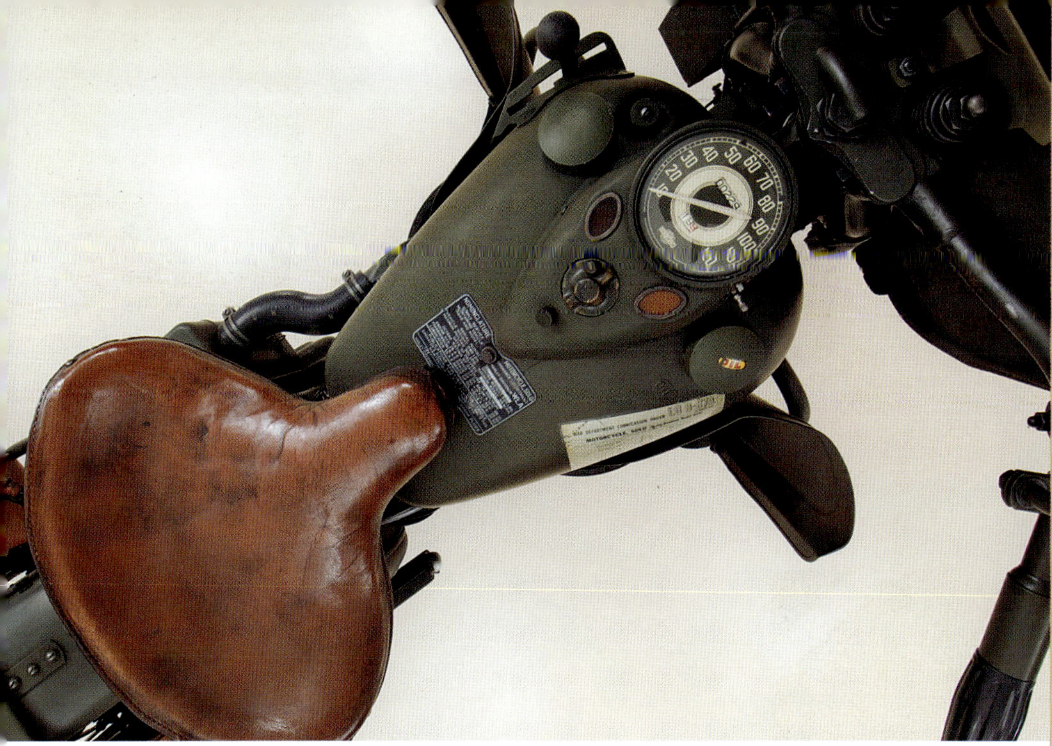

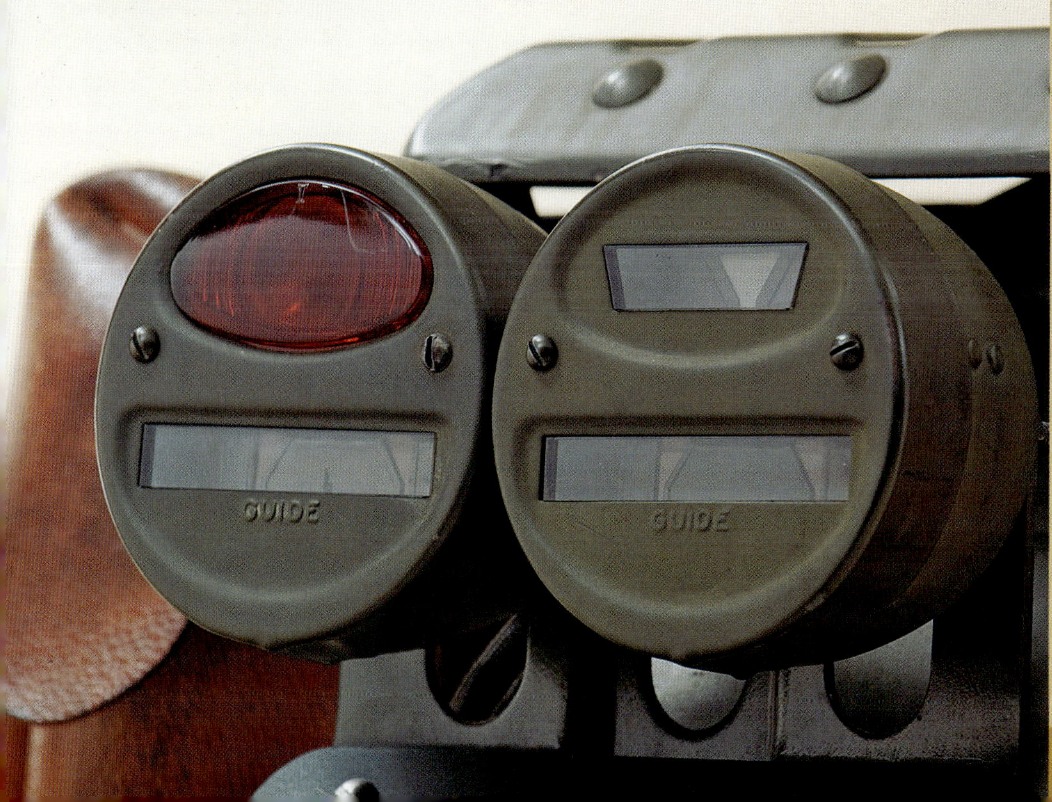
GUIDE
GUIDE

The WLA wasn't the only member of the Harley-Davidson family to serve in the war. The lesser-known Model XA also served, but in a lesser capacity; only 1,100 or so were built before production was suspended.

You might say that the XA was among the hundreds of thousands of conscripts, though, because it was at the U.S. government's request that the model was considered at all. Knowing that the Axis's armed forces would have to be driven out of North Africa before an Allied invasion of the European continent could be carried out, the U.S. War Department asked Harley-Davidson to develop a motorcycle that was suitable for

maneuvering in the hot, sandy desert. Rather than reinvent the wheel, Harley engineers based their design on the German army's BMW. The opposed horizontal twin-cylinder engine easily allowed for an enclosed driveshaft, and cooling the engine was made easier because the cylinders protruded into the wind stream.

But the XA was costly to manufacture, and with the North African campaign nearing a positive end (we won!), production of the German-like model all but ceased. Even so, Harley-Davidson's engineers learned some valuable lessons, among them how to incorporate foot-shifting into the transmission; this was the first foot-shift Harley ever made.

1942 MODEL XA

Price: $870.35
Engine Displacement: 45 cubic inches
Engine Bore & Stroke: 3.125x3.125 inches
Weight: 538 pounds
Wheelbase: 58.75 inches
Wheel Size (F/R): 18/18 inches
Top Speed: 65 miles per hour
Number Produced: 1,100

Did You Know?
The XA was one of the most unorthodox Harley-Davidson designs to come out of Milwaukee. Shaft drive, wet sump lubrication, an integral transmission, and opposed cylinder placement are among the bike's more unusual characteristics.

On the license plate: 42-XA FOR U.S. ARMY

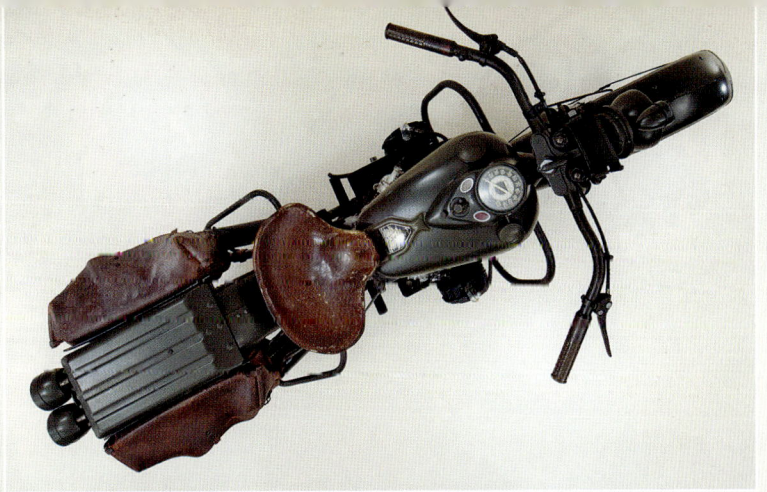

1942
XA

1942 MODEL XA

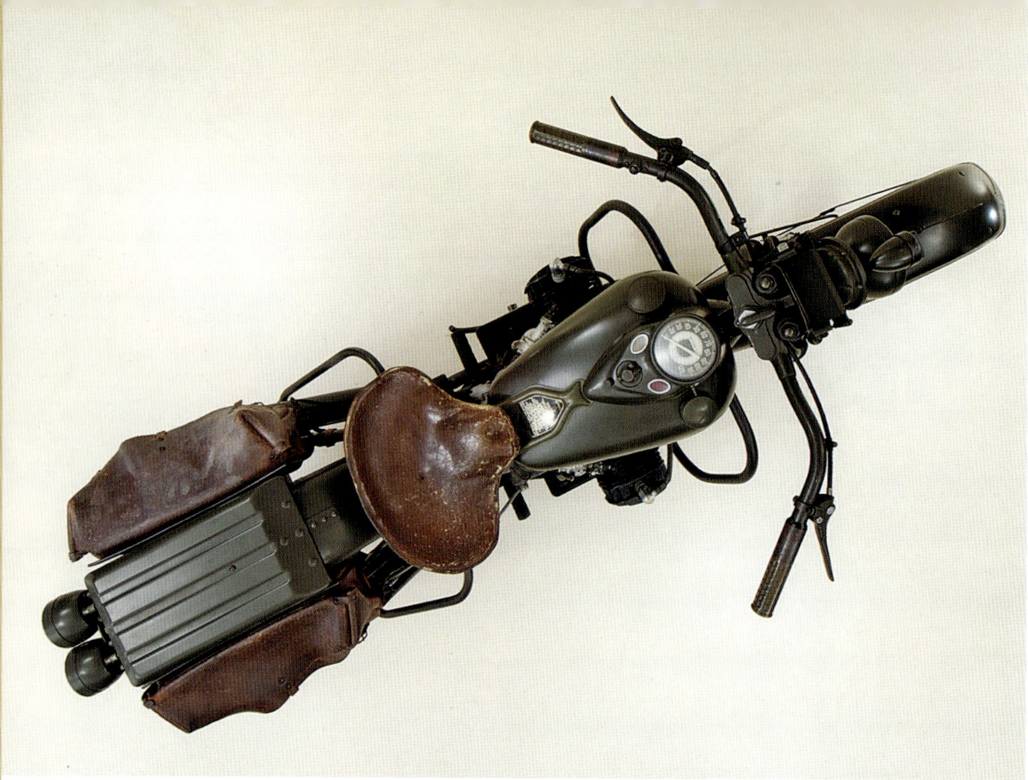

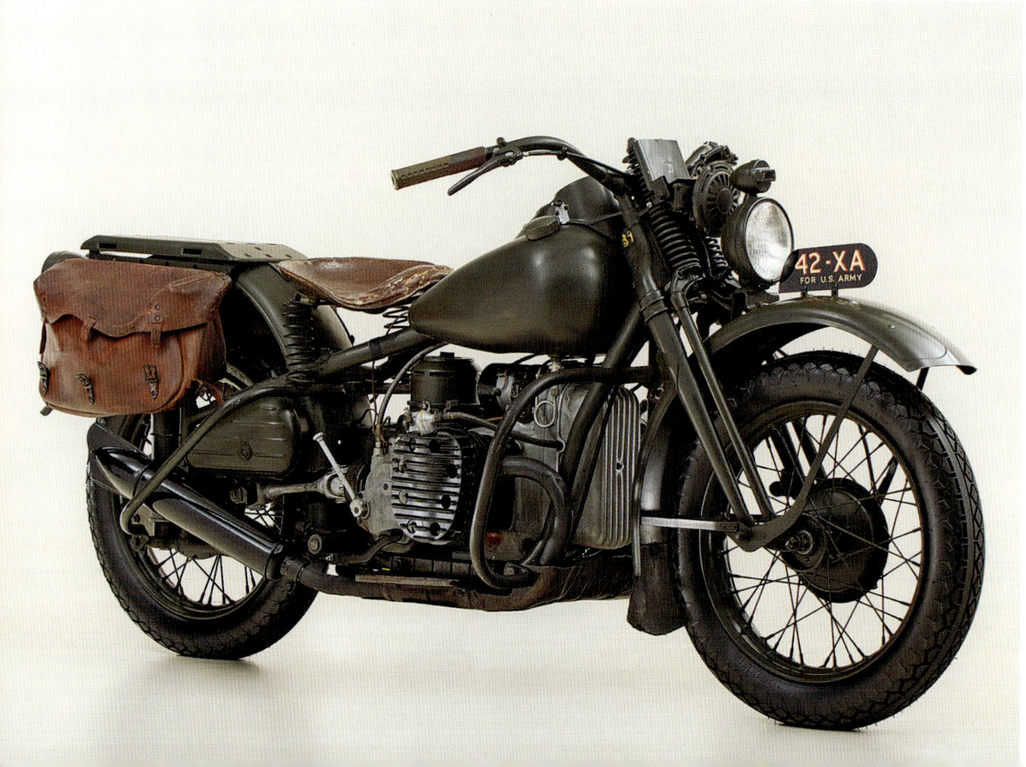

A motorcycle with two-wheel drive? Well, yeah, thanks to a collaborative effort by Harley-Davidson Motor Company, the U.S. War Department, and a scoundrel named Adolf Hitler. When the Allies decided to chase Hitler's army out of North Africa during World War II, the good guys (that would be the Allies) knew that it would require some unconventional weaponry to overcome the adverse conditions presented by the hot, arid desert that constitutes most of the landscape in that part of the Mediterranean Sea region.

One idea was this sidecar rig that Harley-Davidson experimented with, basing it on the Model XA. In this case, the model was designated the XS, the "S" presumably standing for sidecar. In any case, only three of these prototypes were made, and the rig's most outstanding feature has to be the axle and universal joints that deliver power to the motorcycle's rear wheel and the sidecar's

wheel. The ingenious design gave the XS maximum traction while traversing loose sand. The tractor-tread balloon tires were an added bonus, allowing the three-wheel rig to disperse its footprint more evenly over the loose terrain.

Harley-Davidson's archive records show that only three of these rigs were made. Perhaps Hitler's guys lost the battle before the XS could be enlisted to do its share of the fighting. Regardless, the can-do spirit that

this three-wheel, two-man fighting machine represented is another example of why the Allies won the war.

1942 MODEL XS

Price: NA
Horsepower: 23
Engine Displacement: 45 cubic inches
Engine Bore & Stroke: 3.125x3.125 inches
Wheelbase: 58.75 inches
Wheel Size (F/R): 16/16 inches
Number Produced: 3

Did You Know?

The two scabbards on the XS's fork held a Thompson .45-caliber submachine gun and an M-1 carbine, making this one of the most heavily armed motorcycles in the war.

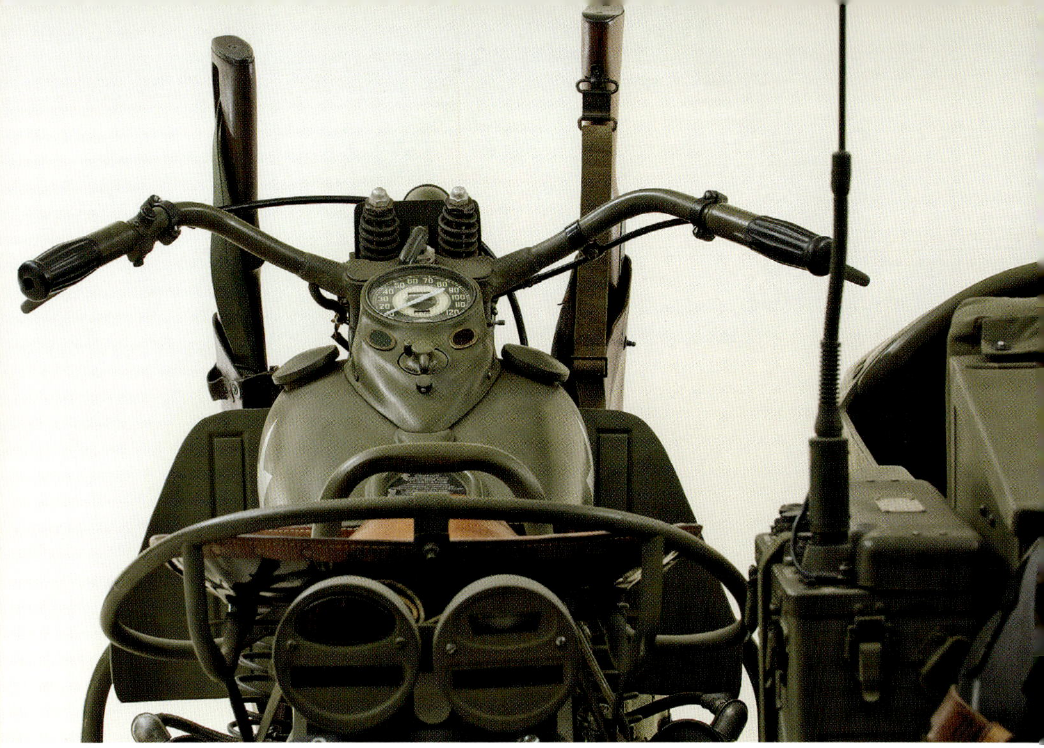

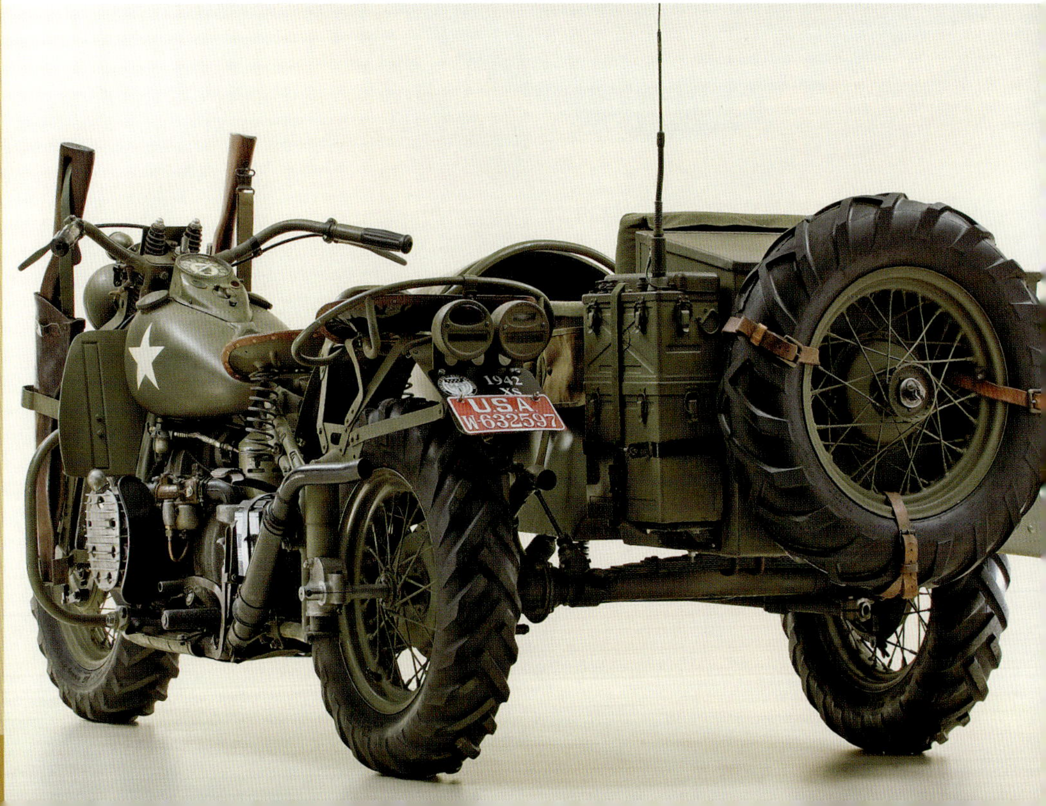
1942
XS
USA
W-632597

Not all of Harley-Davidson's military models went to the U.S. Army. In fact, not all military models were based on the WLA or XA, either. The U.S. Navy had its own idea of what model worked best for its purposes, and one that America's sailors selected was the Model U, introduced as a civilian model in 1937.

Originally, the Model U was intended as a replacement for the V-series 74- and 80-inch flatheads, and the new L-head engine checked in with an enclosed lubrication system; the earlier V engines relied on a flow-through system that sprayed excess oil onto the road (thus the phrase "road oilers"). The Model U's 74-cubic-inch engine was especially useful for sidecar duty, as shown on this combination that served the navy's shore patrol unit. Model Us were also handy for quick transportation by the Seabees (a nickname for construction battalions, or CBs), who were entrusted with building frontline air fields, harbors, and land bases, especially in the Pacific war theater.

Did You Know?

While most of the 90,000-plus motorcycles that Harley-Davidson produced for the military during World War II were based on the venerable WLA, the Model U served the allies, too.

As with all military models, this Model U with sidecar had a small blackout light, in this case mounted on its nonvalance front fender. The siren was handy when rushing to emergency calls, and the rig was painted matte gray, a color familiar to most U.S. Navy ships. All ashore that's going ashore!

1942 MODEL U WITH SIDECAR

Price: NA
Horsepower: 22
Engine Displacement: 74 cubic inches
Wheel Size (F/R): 16/16 inches
Number Produced: NA

Among the first orders of business following Japan's surrender in 1945 was to redirect America's industries toward the civilian sector. And for Harley-Davidson that meant ramping up production of the overhead-valve Model EL (61 cubic inches) and FL (74 cubic inches). This was especially welcomed news for Harley's customers, who had only enjoyed a brief taste of the larger FL when it was introduced in 1941. Records show that 4,452 FLs were built that year, but

1946 MODEL FL

Price: $465
Horsepower: 48
Engine Displacement: 74 cubic inches
Engine Bore & Stroke: 3.43x3.50 inches
Weight: 575 pounds
Wheelbase: 59.5 inches
Wheel Size (F/R): 16/16 inches
Top Speed: 95 miles per hour
Number Produced: 3,986

production dwindled significantly each of the following four years due to the war; 619 rolled off the assembly line in 1945, but that number swelled to 3,986 the next year when this blue edition was built.

And it was a good thing that this FL's blue paint is so striking. In an effort to help the war-torn countries in Europe and Asia rebuild, their industries were given priority for many raw materials, among them rubber, steel, and fuel, even chromium. As such, many early postwar Harleys lacked the abundance of chromed parts identified with the brand today. Colorful paint jobs helped give those early peacetime bikes a true nonmilitary appearance.

There was another bonus when the war was over—Harley-Davidson engineers could once again devote their energies to improving their products. Customers would find this out in 1948 when a revamped FL engine would be employed.

Did You Know?

Due to the scarcity of chrome, early 1946 Harley-Davidson engines had their tappet guides painted silver. By the end of the model year, chrome was more abundant and began to appear on various components.

1946 MODEL FL

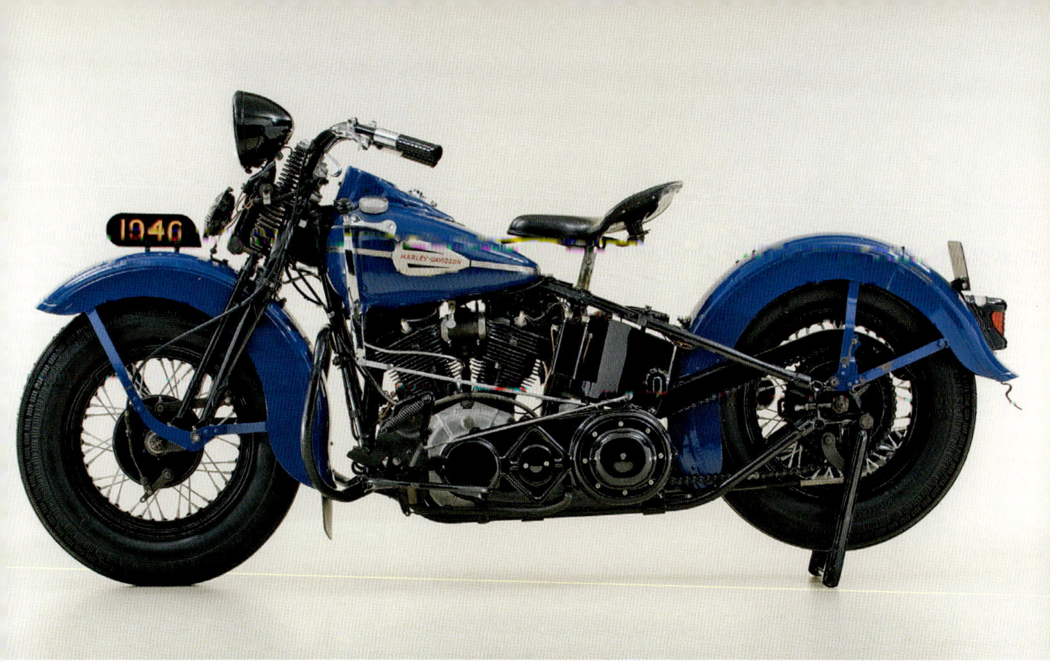

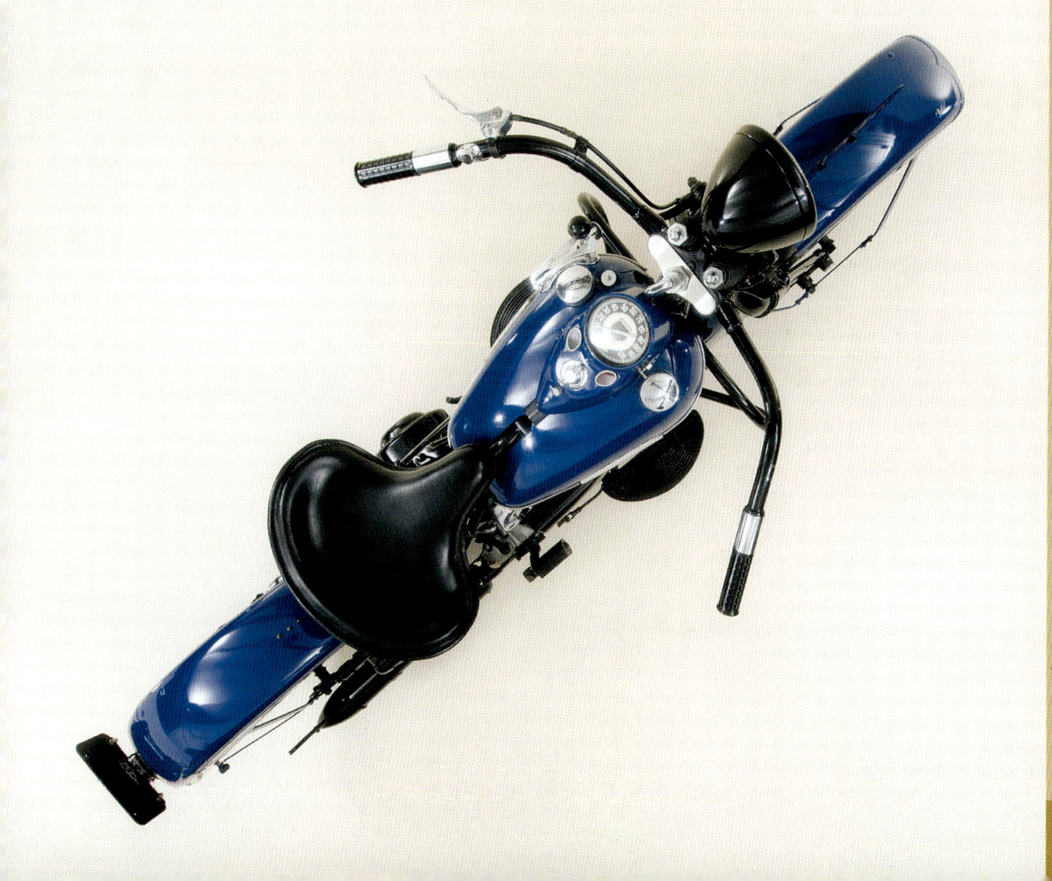

CHAPTER 3
POSTWAR PROGRESS

People who grew up during the 1950s will argue that the Ike Era, as that decade was called, was perhaps the best time to be an American. The country was basking in unparalleled prosperity, yet our society still enjoyed much of the innocence that marked past years when immigrants flocked to these shores to pursue the Great American Dream.

Part of that dream included riding great American motorcycles, and it was during the immediate postwar era that Harley-Davidson introduced some of its most provocative models. Among the new breed were the Panhead (an updated version of the Model E, or Knucklehead, Big Twin), the Model K (an improved variation of the 45-cubic-inch Model W), the Sportster (the overhead-valve successor to the Model K), and the Aermacchi Sprint (Harley-Davidson's first import model).

By 1966, the social climate in America was experiencing change. Harley-Davidson experienced a metamorphosis of its own, too. Electric starters were becoming a common fixture on most models, suspension upgrades were introduced across the board, and the Motor Company even got a new owner—American Machine and Foundry.

Yet through it all, one thing remained constant: Harley owners remained loyal to the brand. And that, among all other factors, was critical to the Motor Company's survival in coming years.

Most of the attention given to the 1948 FL by enthusiasts today is focused on the engine. Rightfully so, because the 1948 FL was an improved variation of Harley's original 1936 overhead-valve model. The updated engine had hydraulic lifters for a quieter, more precise valvetrain, and the new aluminum cylinder heads had reshaped exhaust ports, a new intake manifold, and pressed-steel rocker covers that eventually contributed to the engine's nickname—Panhead. More aluminum than ever was incorporated into this engine's overall design, the result being a Big Twin that weighed about 8 pounds less than the Knucklehead that it replaced.

But there was more to the new model than just a revamped engine. The new FL's

1948 MODEL FL

Price: $650
Horsepower: 50
Engine Displacement: 74 cubic inches
Weight: 565 pounds
Wheelbase: 59.5 inches
Wheel Size (F/R): 16/16 inches
Top Speed: 100 miles per hour
Number Produced: 8,071

frame lugs were improved for a more rigid assembly, and the rider's seat was given Latex-filled padding for a more comfortable ride. Extra chrome brightened up the entire bike, and a multi-plate clutch assembly was advertised to offer smoother operation and longer life.

While it appeared that Harley-Davidson was prepared to move forward with this new model, two familiar fixtures were about to be dropped for 1949: The 74-cubic-inch flathead—the Model U—was in its final year for 1948, and the leading-link springer fork was destined to be replaced by an all-new hydraulic unit for 1949.

Did You Know?

While the Panhead, as enthusiasts eventually labeled the updated overhead-valve engine, broke new ground for Harley-Davidson in 1948, that was the final year for the 74-cubic-inch Model U flathead.

1948 MODEL FL

One of the attractions that Harley-Davidson motorcycles offer owners is flexibility for customization. And perhaps the favorite model to customize is the Big Twin. One person who recognized that early on was James M. Kobe, who bought this FL new in 1948. Over the years, Kobe did what many Harley owners have done to their bikes—he personalized the FL to suit his riding needs.

To power the extra lighting that he added, Kobe converted the electrics to a 12-volt system, mounting an alternator to the engine case. Hidden behind those early-day leather saddlebags is a belt-drive system that he adapted from a late-model Sportster. The belt is quieter, cleaner, and in certain ways, more trouble-free than the roller chain it replaced. A variety of automotive gauges were mounted to a homemade dash that shrouds the handlebar, and a quick glance at the seat's skirts lets you know right away who owns this bike.

Kobe rode his 1948 FL to the 95th Anniversary Homecoming in June 1998, and when he rolled into Milwaukee, the bike's odometer registered slightly more than 100,000 miles. Two months later, he donated the bike to the Motor Company for its growing archive collection. It had been quite a ride for James M. Kobe and his 1948 FL.

1948 MODEL FL CUSTOM

Price: $650
Horsepower: 50
Engine Displacement: 74 cubic inches
Wheel Size (F/R): 16/16 inches
Top Speed: 100 miles per hour
Number Produced: 8,071

Did You Know?

During the time that James Kobe owned his 1948 FL (he presented the bike to the Motor Company in August 1998), 10 presidents had lived in the White House.

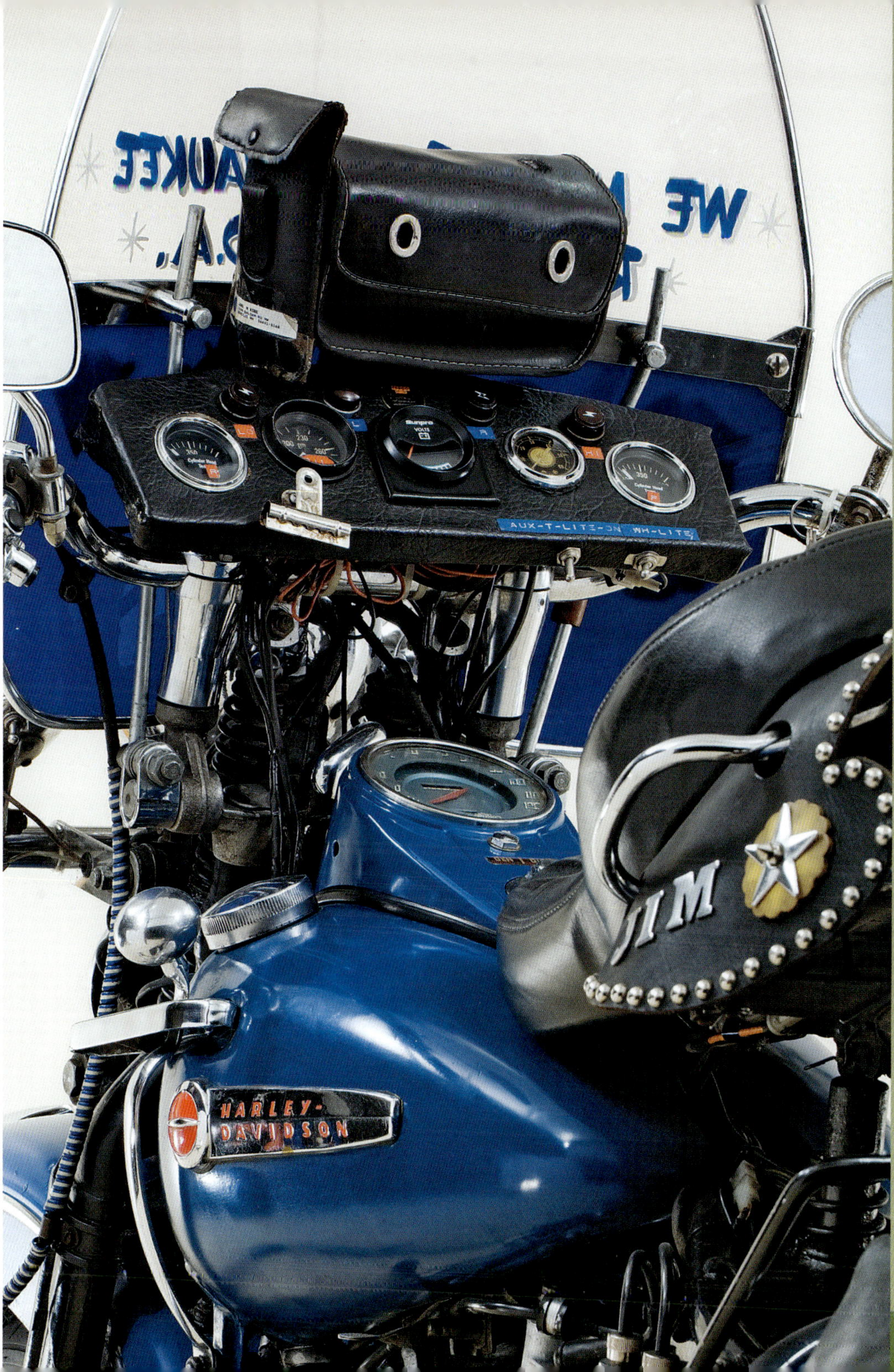

1948 MODEL FL CUSTOM

Not all Harley-Davidsons have V-twin engines. In fact, not all Harley-Davidsons have four-stroke engines. Case in point is the Model S, a bike powered by a single-cylinder 125cc two-stroke engine.

Harley-Davidson based the diminutive S's design on the German-built DKW RT125. As part of the war reparations, England and America gained patent rights to this little two-cycle engine. Birmingham Small Arms (BSA) built the British version, calling it the Bantam. On this side of the Atlantic Ocean, Harley-Davidson offered its own variation,

1948 MODEL S

Price: $325
Horsepower: 2
Engine Displacement: 125cc
Wheelbase: 50 inches
Wheel Size (F/R): 19/19 inches
Seat Height: 27.5 inches
Number Produced: 10,117

called the Model S. Harley's Model S produced about 2 horsepower and had a foot-shift three-speed transmission. The

tiddler engine was reputed to get 90 miles to the gallon, a good thing because gasoline had to be premixed with oil before putting it into the 1.75-gallon gas tank.

The original Model S had a rigid frame that relied on a girder-style fork to help soak up bumps for the front tire. Later versions were equipped with hydraulic forks. The engine also received updates, and by 1953 a 165cc version was offered. That basic package remained in the lineup until 1963, when the BTH Scat replaced it. The Scat was intended more for off-road use and had rear suspension among other modern upgrades. The engine's displacement was increased again in 1966, when the 175cc BTH Bobcat hit the dealer showroom floors. From tiny acorns mighty oaks grow.

Did You Know?
Despite being the smallest model in Harley-Davidson's lineup for 1948, the diminutive two-stroke was the company's biggest seller, surpassing the FL by more than 2,000 units sold.

During the first half of the twentieth century, Harley-Davidson seldom used official names to denote various models. That changed in 1949 with an updated FL, Harley's first Big Twin to use a hydraulically damped fork. Fittingly, Harley introduced the new model as the Hydra-Glide. The Hydra-Glide's tubular fork legs contained coil springs and hydraulic fluid (oil) that flowed through orifices in rods to help

dampen spring movement for an improved and more comfortable ride.

The new fork brought with it a larger and better front brake, too. The internal-expanding mechanical drum brake measured 8 inches in diameter. And to further boost rider comfort, a rubber-mounted handlebar was included on the accessory list, as was the option to replace the new fork with the tried-and-tested leading-link springer fork used on

previous Big Twins. As you might guess, few customers opted for that second option.

The Hydra-Glide established the iconic Harley look for years to come, and when the new Evolution engine was mounted into a revolutionary Softail frame for 1984, Harley Davidson stylists used the 1949 Hydra-Glide's lines as their template. *That's* how significant this model is to current and future Harley owners.

1949 MODEL FL HYDRA-GLIDE

Price: $750
Horsepower: 55
Engine Displacement: 74 cubic inches
Weight: 500 pounds
Wheelbase: 59.5 inches
Wheel Size (F/R): 16/16 inches
Top Speed: 100 miles per hour
Number Produced: 8,014

Did You Know?

The leading-link springer fork was still available as an option on all E and F models, but few customers ordered it.

1949

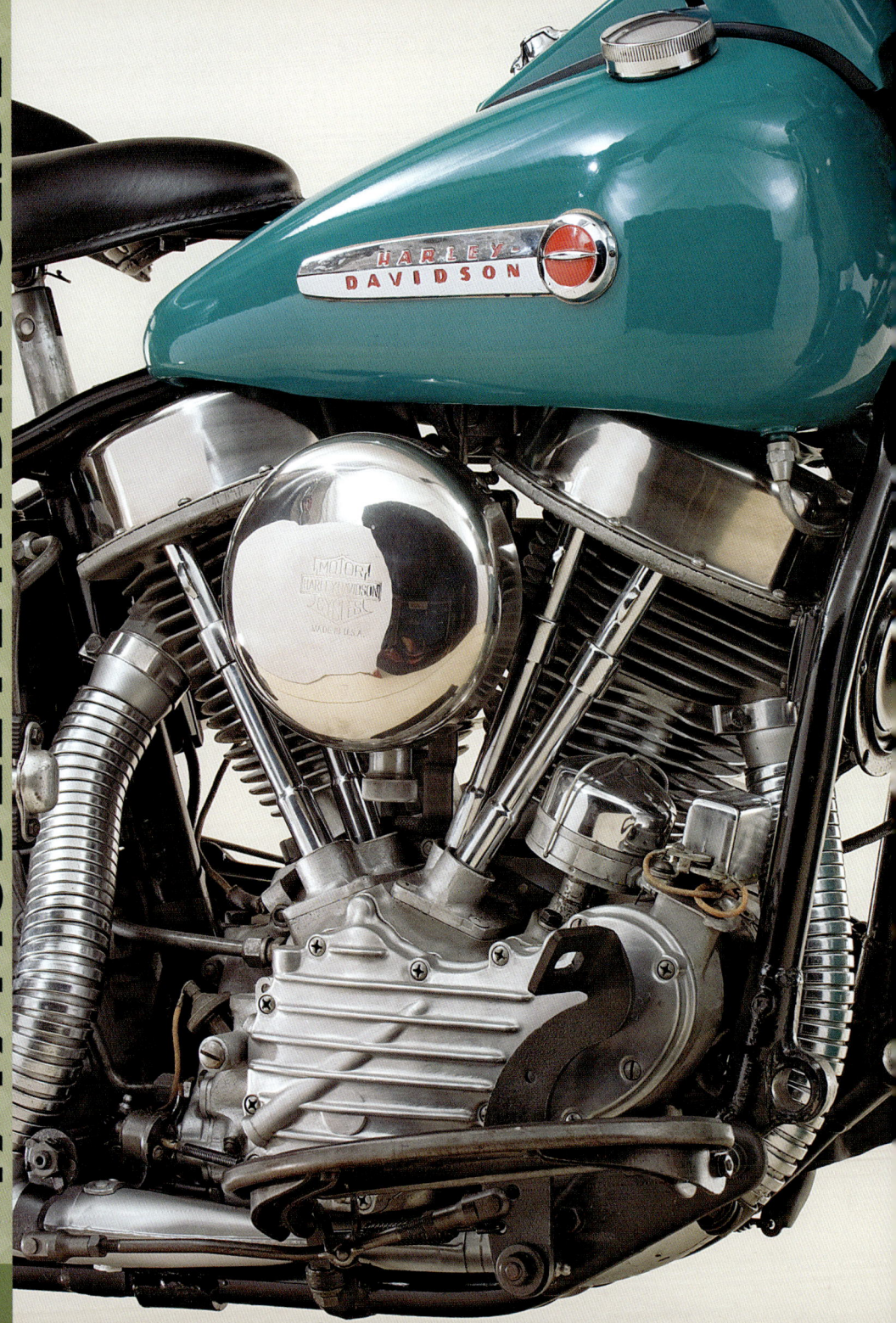

Before there was a Honda motorcycle, or even motorcycles bearing the names Kawasaki or Suzuki, there was Rikuo. And if the red Rikuo shown here looks familiar, it's because this Japanese motorcycle brand was developed using blueprints and tooling that Harley-Davidson supplied during the early 1930s. You might say that the Rikuo was the original Japanese-built Harley clone.

The Rikuo story begins with an American entrepreneur named Alfred Richard Child. As part of Harley-Davidson's move to

expand its markets in foreign countries, the H-D Motorcycle Sales Company of Japan had been established in 1924, and Child was involved with marketing the American bikes on Japanese soil. Eventually, Child saw an opportunity for Harley-Davidson to license Sankyo Pharmaceuticals to manufacture Harleys in its own country, all but negating the need to import the American made bikes to Japan. By 1935, the Shinagawa factory was producing its own versions of the W, and later U, models.

Rikuo continued manufacturing motorcycles after World War II and was a major supplier of bikes to Japanese police departments through the 1960s. The big-inch, low-compression, V-twin engines worked well on the crowded streets of Tokyo and other large cities.

1952 RIKUO (BASED ON 1945 WL SPECS)

Price: NA
Engine Displacement: 45 cubic inches
Engine Bore & Stroke: 2.75x3.81 inches
Weight: 540 pounds
Wheelbase: 57.5 inches
Wheel Size (F/R): 16/16 inches
Top Speed: 65 miles per hour
Number Produced: NA

Did You Know?

Eventually Rikuo went out of business, one of the first motorcycle companies to succumb to the fledgling new Japanese motorcycle industry that evolved from the 1960s.

Okay, we'll get the celebrity name-dropping thing out of the way so we can move on to talk about the bike: This is the same Harley-Davidson that appeared on the May 1956 cover of *The Enthusiast* with a young Elvis Presley on the saddle, doffing his hat to the camera. The King owned the Pepper Red and white bike for about a year before he stepped up to buy a 1957 FL.

More to the point, Presley's 1956 Model KH represented one of 539 KHs that the Motor Company built to satisfy a growing hunger among American motorcycle enthusiasts for a high-performance machine. The K series was introduced in 1952, and it carried with it a few interesting features never used on a Harley-Davidson motorcycle before. For starters, the original Model K's

45-cubic-inch flathead engine had an integral four-speed, foot-shift transmission. This necessitated a hand-operated clutch lever on the left-hand grip, and the K's hydraulically damped rear swingarm was also a first among the Milwaukee-built bikes.

Two years later, the Model K's engine displacement was increased to 55 cubic inches, and with the change came a new name—the Model KH. Larger valves, reshaped port chambers in the cylinder heads, new pistons, and higher compression translated to about a 12 percent horsepower gain. In short, the KH became King of the Road in America. It was truly a bike fit for a King.

1956 MODEL KH

Price: $935
Horsepower: 38
Engine Displacement: 55 cubic inches (883cc)
Engine Bore & Stroke: 2.75x4.56 inches
Weight: 400 pounds
Wheelbase: 56.5 inches
Wheel Size (F/R): 19/19 inches
Top Speed: 95 miles per hour
Number Produced: 539

Did You Know?

Joe Leonard won the first AMA Grand National Championship Series in 1954 riding a KR, which was based on the Model K. Prior to 1954, the AMA champion was determined at a single race, the Springfield Mile.

1956
KH ELVIS

1956 MODEL KH

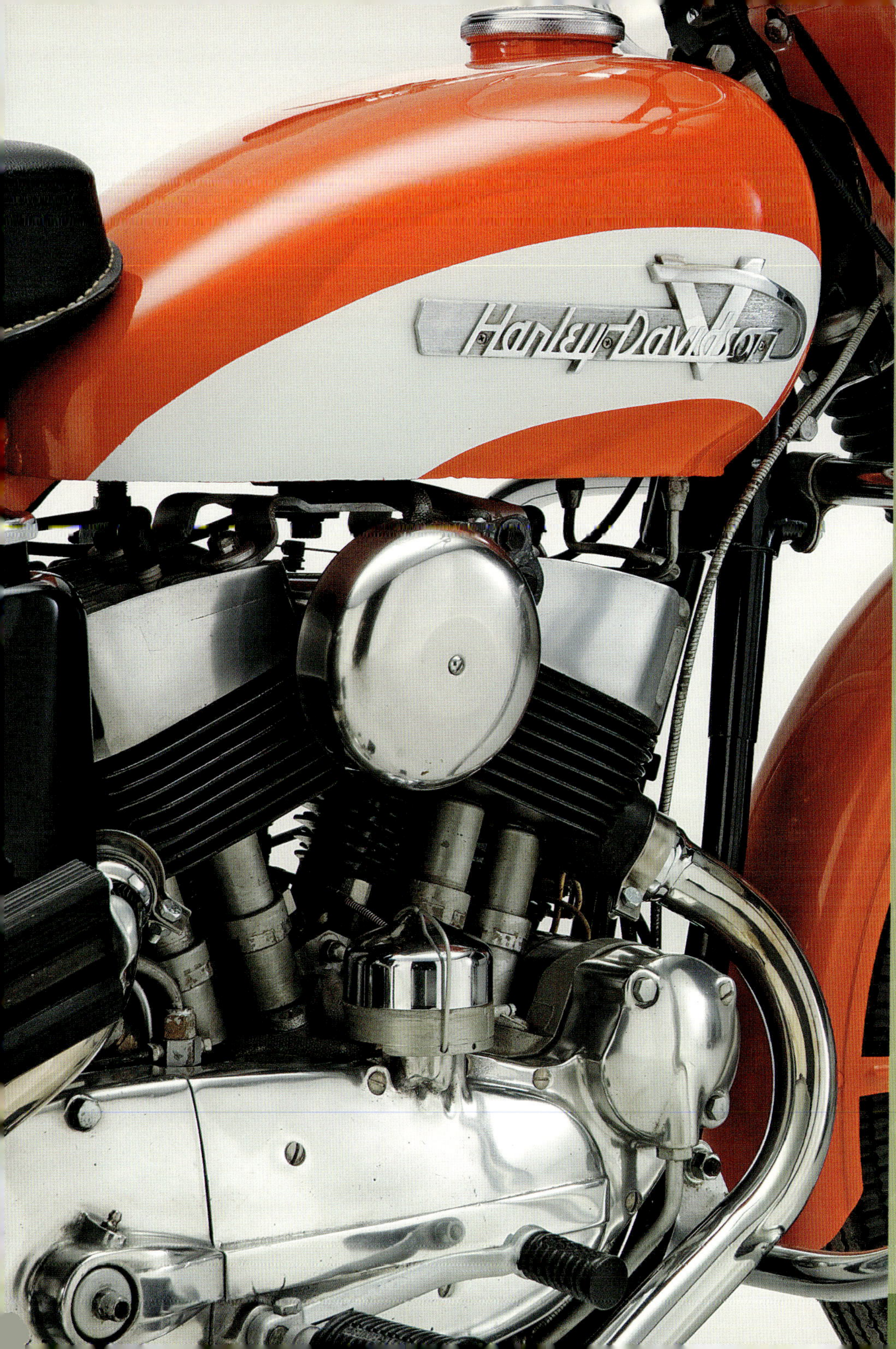

"Say, if you're looking for a real surprise in performance, stop in at your Harley-Davidson Dealer's and take a spin on the 'Sportster'—a 55-'cubic'-inch package of dynamite from Milwaukee." So wrote editor Bill Bagnall in the opening sentence of his road test of the all-new 1957 XL Sportster for the March 1957 issue of *Motorcyclist* magazine.

The 1957 Sportster wasn't necessarily an all-new design—its chassis was based on the 1956 KH that it replaced—but its engine represented a noticeable leap forward for Harley-Davidson. Gone was the KH flathead, and in its place was a new, more powerful overhead engine. The new OHV engine's compression ratio was set at 9:1, good for 40 horsepower at 5,500 rpm.

No doubt, the Sportster was built for sport, and to prove its mettle, Harley-Davidson dealer Gerald McGovern rode a stock XL for the 1957 Jack Pine Enduro in Michigan, and won. His success obviously encouraged the Motor Company to concentrate on making its new XL a contender wherever it went, and the following year three more variations hit the market. The XLH, XLC, and XLCH models had engines with higher compression ratios and other modifications, making them suitable for a variety of competition categories. Riders aboard competitors' brands in 1958 were truly in for a surprise, the likes of which even Bill Bagnall didn't foresee in early 1957.

1957 MODEL XL SPORTSTER

Price: $1,103
Horsepower: 40
Engine Displacement: 55 cubic inches (883cc)
Engine Bore & Stroke: 3.00x3.81 inches
Weight: 495 pounds
Wheelbase: 57 inches
Wheel Size (F/R): 18/18 inches
Top Speed: 95 miles per hour
Number Produced: 1,983

Did You Know?

The shorter stroke XL engine revved much quicker than the K, the engine that it replaced. It also made more power thanks to its overhead-valve design with hemispherical combustion chambers, larger valves, and new camshaft configurations.

Much has been written and said about the two original *Easy Rider* bikes, some of it fact, some of it fiction. Regardless, nobody can dispute that the two iconic custom choppers from that movie deserved as much acclaim as the stars—Peter Fonda and Dennis Hopper—who rode them.

Both of the *Easy Rider* bikes were based on early-vintage Panheads, which were rather plentiful at the time that builders Ben Hardy and Cliff Vaughs chopped them for the 1969 movie. In reality, Hardy and Vaughs supplied two of each bike to minimize downtime while filming. If one bike needed repair, its twin could stand in during filming.

1957 MODEL FLH "BILLY" BIKE REPLICA

Price: NA
Engine Displacement: 74 cubic inches
Engine Bore & Stroke: 3.44x3.97 inches
Wheel Size (F/R): 21/16 inches
Number Produced: 2

Unfortunately, one of the choppers was wrecked during the movie's production and the remaining three were stolen shortly after the final wrap, so little is really known about the originals other than they were based on rigid-frame Harleys from the 1950s. Shown here is a replica of Hopper's bike, built by Jim Beck of Pomona, California.

Of the two bikes, the Billy Bike, as Dennis Hopper's mount became known, is perhaps the more conservative in design and concept. According to Fonda, this was done for a reason—Hopper wasn't an experienced rider, so his movie bike didn't have the radical raked steering head and extended fork as did Fonda's Captain America bike.

But the Billy Bike's wide-glide front end and more conservative lines set the tone for many choppers to come during the halcyon period after the movie's release. The Billy Bike's formula offered the look of an outlaw bike but with rider-friendly handling.

Did You Know?

Even though two Billy Bikes were built for the movie *Easy Rider*, neither of the originals are known to exist. Even so, countless replicas and tribute Billy Bikes have been made since 1969.

19 CAL 69
BILLY

1957 MODEL FLH "BILLY" BIKE REPLICA

19 CAL 69
BILLY

1958 MODEL FLH

Hot on the heels of the 1957 XL Sportster's successful debut, Harley-Davidson released an improved FLH, the Duo-Glide, for 1958. As the name suggests, the Duo-Glide has suspension for both wheels. Gone is the rigid frame that cradled every Big Twin since 1936, and in its place, the Motor Company rolled out a frame with a hydraulically damped fork and two rear shock absorbers.

The new rear suspension opened the door for a couple other improvements as

1958 MODEL FLH

Price: $1,243
Horsepower: 52
Engine Displacement: 74 cubic inches
Engine Bore & Stroke: 3.44x3.97 inches
Weight: 648 pounds
Wheelbase: 60 inches
Wheel Size (F/R): 16/16 inches
Top Speed: 100 miles per hour
Number Produced: 164

well, chief among them the hydraulic rear brake. A new, rather eye-catching mounting system for the rear fender also bowed—a design feature that became a mainstay on Big Twins.

The FLH ushered in a few more notable changes: The oil tank necessitated a new bracket for the remote oil filter, and the oil return lines were improved. A single two-into-one exhaust pipe was standard, but customers could order a left- and right-side system as an accessory.

Despite the advanced chassis design, some diehard Big Twin riders in 1958 looked at the FLH with skepticism. Rumors of uncontrollable wobbling and skittish behavior in turns were common, but those suspicions proved groundless. In the end, the FLH Duo-Glide gained a reputation for what it was—a smooth, easy-to-ride, long-distance motorcycle.

Did You Know?

Duo-Glide inscription badges were mounted to the sides of the front fender to let people know the bike was special in 1958. To this day, the same badge placement is used on various Big Twin models.

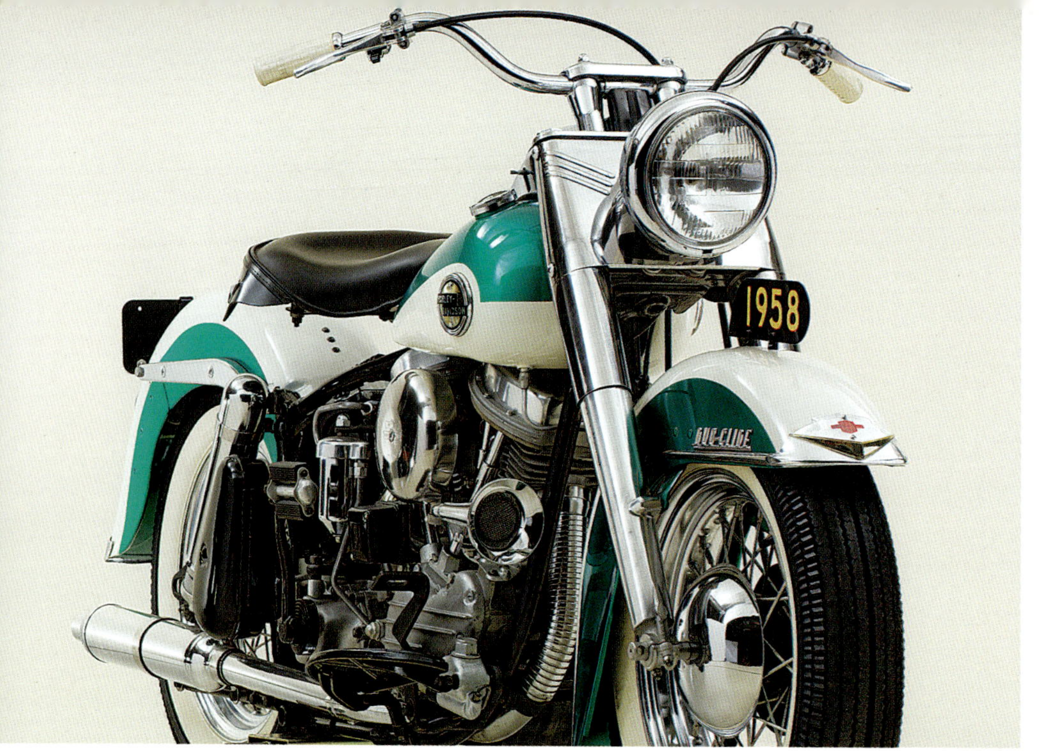
1958

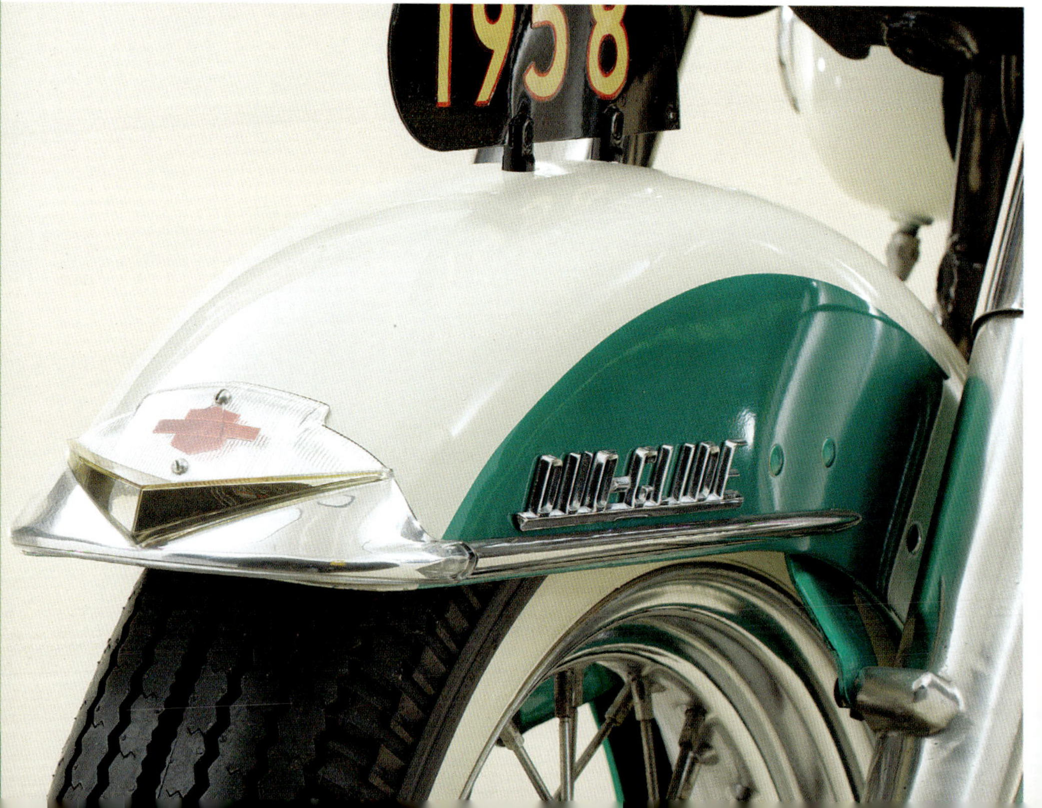
DUO-GLIDE

Say the word "chopper," and chances are that an image of the Captain America bike from the 1969 movie *Easy Rider* will pop up in your mind. For no other motorcycle had an impact on the American chopper movement of the 1970s as great as that of the "Captain America" bike that film star Peter Fonda rode as *Easy Rider*'s main character, Wyatt, a.k.a., "Captain America."

1960 MODEL FLH CAPTAIN AMERICA

Price: NA
Engine Displacement: 74 cubic inches
Engine Bore & Stroke: 3.44x3.97 inches
Wheel Size (F/R): 21/16 inches
Number Produced: 2

The bike's signature is its red, white, and blue peanut gas tank perched atop an all-chrome rigid frame. In fact, the gas tank is about the only thing on the bike that *isn't* chrome plated! Many of the Panhead engine's parts were dipped in the chroming vat, and the fork legs and foot and hand controls were plated, too. Even the banana seat's black upholstery is festooned with chromed buttons.

Although the original bike is said to have disappeared, many replicas have been made in tribute to Fonda's ride. Jim Beck of Pomona, California, built this particular Captain America replica for the Otis Chandler Vintage Museum. When the Chandler collection was dissolved, the bike found a new home in the H-D Archives in 1999.

Did You Know?

The engine used in the original Captain America bike that Peter Fonda rode in the film *Easy Rider* was from a 1962 police bike. This replica has a 1960 Panhead engine.

1960 MODEL FLH CAPTAIN AMERICA

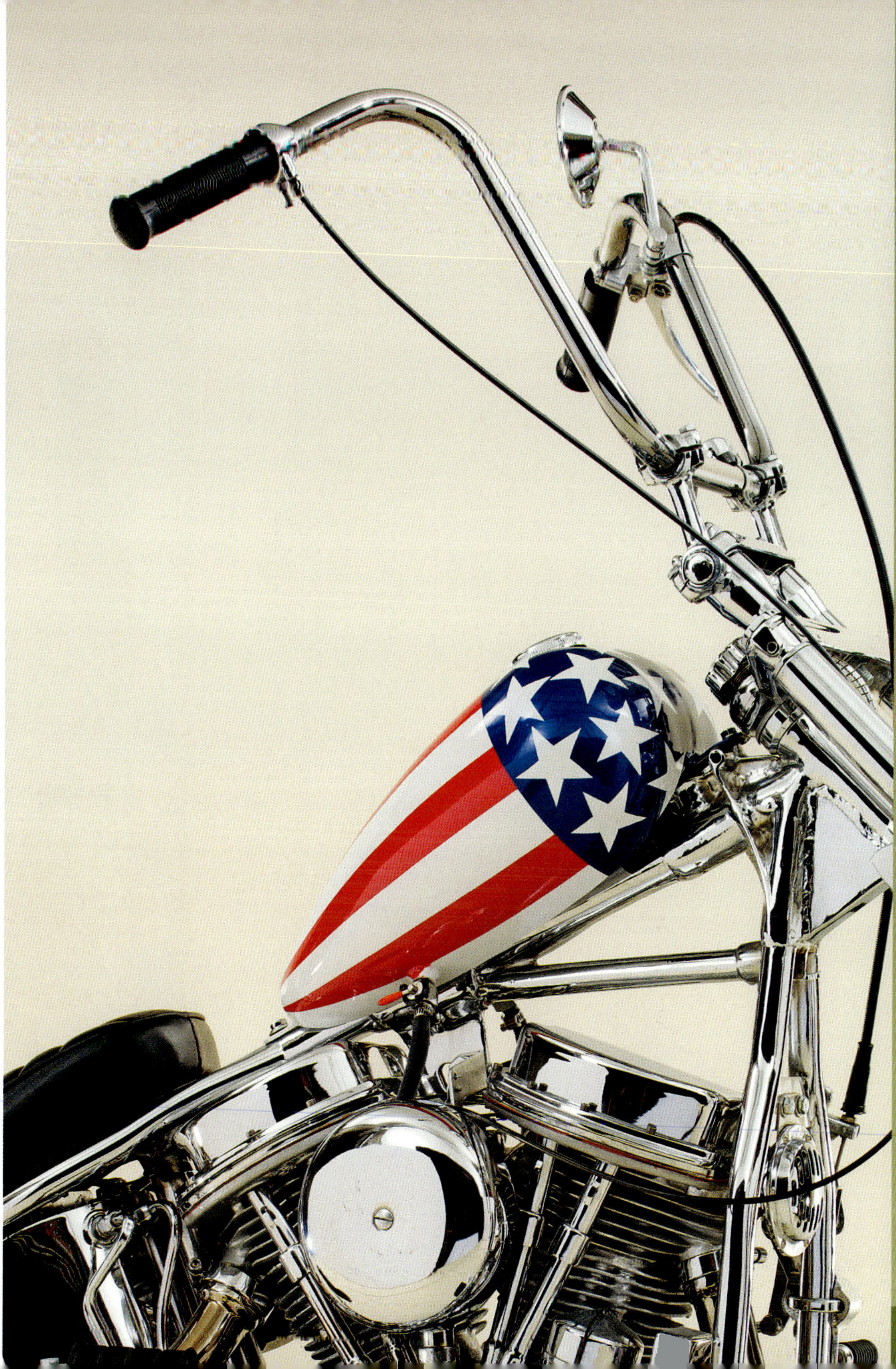

1960 MODEL FLH CAPTAIN AMERICA

A new era for Harley-Davidson began in 1961. That was the first year that the Motor Company began importing bikes from its latest acquisition, the Italian motorcycle company Aermacchi. The first Aermacchi model to reach these shores was the Model C Sprint.

Best known simply as the Sprint, the bike was marketed to fill the gap between Harley-Davidson's small two-stroke models and the Sportster and FLH. The Sprint was

1961 MODEL C SPRINT

Price: $695
Horsepower: 18
Engine Displacement: 15 cubic inches (250cc)
Engine Bore & Stroke: 2.59x2.83 inches
Weight: 270 pounds
Wheelbase: 52 inches
Wheel Size (F/R): 17/17 inches
Top Speed: 75 miles per hour

powered by a single-cylinder, 250cc four-stroke engine. The cylinder was positioned horizontally, and its overhead valves were pushrod activated. Compression ratio was 9:1, and the 15-cubic-inch engine produced a claimed 18 horsepower at 7,500 rpm.

The Sprint was a bit unorthodox compared to most bikes sold in America at the time. The kick-start lever was positioned on the bike's left side, and the side stand was on the right side.

A race-only version, the CRTT, was also offered, and by 1962 a second street model was available. The CH Sprint had an engine equipped with a larger carburetor and more compression, delivering 21 horsepower. The Sprint underwent various changes and improvements through the years, including larger displacement (350cc) in 1969. Even so, its aging design made it obsolete, and by 1975 it was replaced with a two-stroke, single-cylinder 250 (SS for the street and SX for off-road use).

Did You Know?

Variations of the Sprint remained in Harley-Davidson's lineup for 13 years. The engine size eventually grew to 350cc.

1961 MODEL C SPRINT

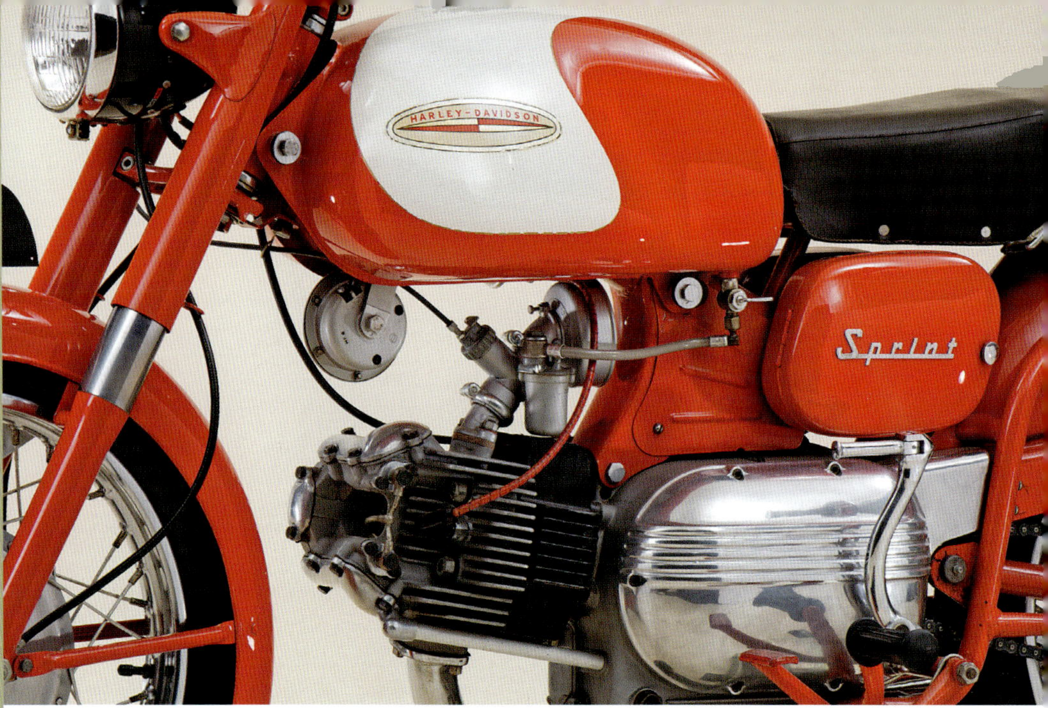

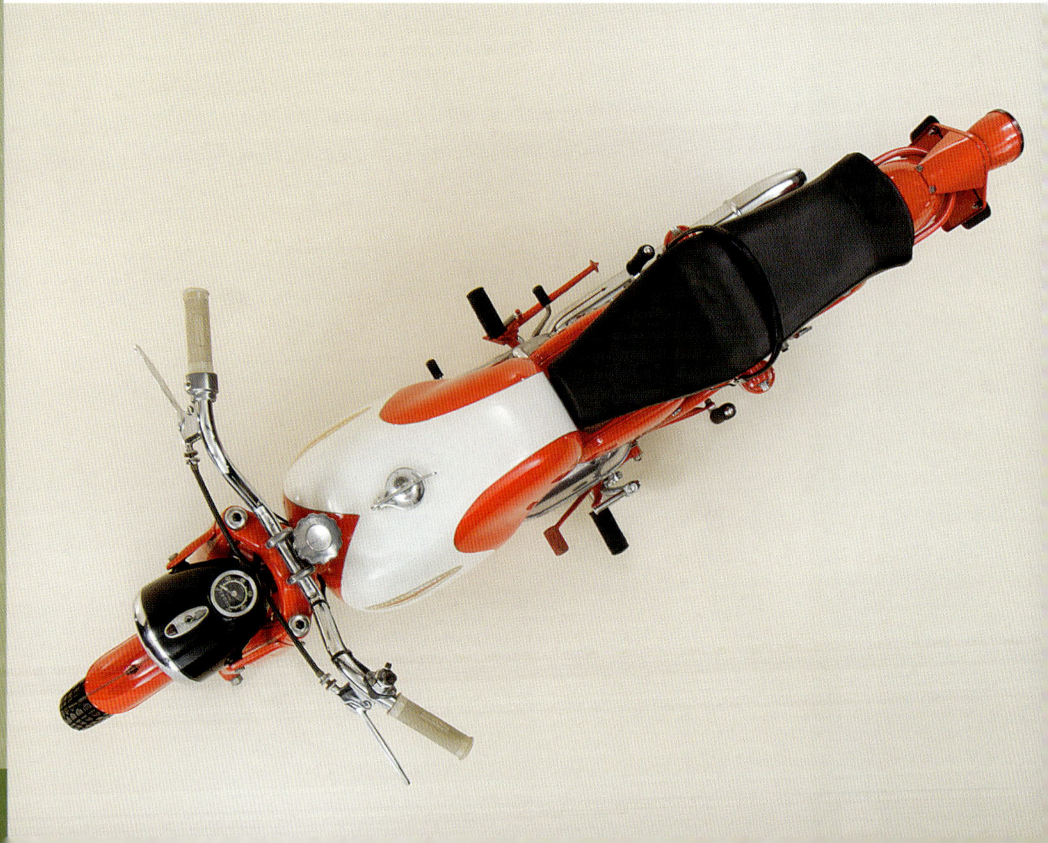

1961
C

Harley-Davidson customers looking to buy a new FLH were greeted with a few surprises for 1965. Foremost, the Panhead engine was given an electric starter, which necessitated a few modifications as well. First, a strong cast-aluminum primary case was adapted to withstand the torque from the electric starter motor. Next, to power the starter motor, electrics were upgraded from 6 volts to 12 volts, which required a larger battery. To make room, the familiar horseshoe battery box/oil tank was replaced with a new rectangular oil tank on the left side, and the larger battery sat on the right. Finally, to designate that this was an electric-start model, the letter "B" was added to the FLH nomenclature and remained through 1970.

1965 MODEL FLHB ELECTRA-GLIDE WITH MODEL LE SIDECAR

Price: Sidecar prices vary
Wheel Size: 16 inches
Number Produced: Based on demand

Did You Know?

Sidecars have been listed among Harley-Davidson's accessories and optional items since the early years of the company. In *Cycle Guide* magazine's September 1979 cover story about a Harley-Davidson sidecar, the editors described the three-wheeler as "a rare bit of glamour and frivolity for a humdrum world."

The FLHB shown here carries a Model LE sidecar. Interestingly, because this FLHB has a hand-shifter, its gas tank is not the 5-gallon fuel cell that Harley-Davidson introduced for the 1965 model year. All 1965 FLHBs with the optional hand-shifter retained the 3.5-gallon gas tanks of old.

And speaking of old, by 1965 the Panhead engine was getting long in the tooth, so it was due for replacement. The following model year had even more surprises for Harley customers, which an updated version of the legendary 74-cubic-inch engine would bow. That engine would eventually become known as the Shovelhead.

CHAPTER 4
BIKES AS
BIG BUSINESS

It's been said that the more things change, the more they remain the same. Perhaps that is the case; it certainly was true when American Machine and Foundry acquired Harley-Davidson in 1969—the motorcycles produced by the restructured company remained pretty much the same in the following years. People will argue that quality from that time—known among Harley enthusiasts as the AMF Era—suffered, but the overall scope of the brand remained unchanged.

Despite the corporate upheaval, the famous Bar & Shield emblem could be found on some interesting—even landmark—models during the time. Among the bikes to wear the AMF/Harley-Davidson logo were the FX Super Glide, the XLCR Café Racer, the FXB Sturgis, and the FXS Low Rider, to name a few.

But to quote another oft-used phrase, what goes around comes around. And in 1981, Harley-Davidson ownership came around once again to the folks in Milwaukee, when 13 executives of the company boldly bought out AMF's shares of stock in the Motor Company. On June 13, 1981, the battle cry in Milwaukee became "The Eagle soars alone." A new era was unfolding for America's premier motorcycle manufacturer.

Despite a company cash crisis and an attempted hostile takeover by Bangor Punta Corporation (a diversified holding company), Harley-Davidson Motor Company pressed on in 1968 with the business of selling its motorcycles. An updated Big Twin engine had been introduced in 1966, and this powerplant became known to enthusiasts as the Shovelhead. Like the update of 1948, the new engine had a reconfigured top end that gave it a fresh look as well. A new oil pump with an aluminum body and a wet-plate clutch were also among the changes for 1968. More appropriately, the addition of an electric starter in 1965 gave rise to the name Electra Glide, replacing Duo-Glide for the FL line.

The changes were heralded by Harley-Davidson's advertisements of the time as a bike that offered "the smoothest ride in the industry." Harley's Big Twin models also showcased a lot of chromed parts and accessories. The model featured here includes the much-heralded King of the Highway Group, plus the Chrome Finish

1968 MODEL FLHFB ELECTRA GLIDE

Price: $1,800
Horsepower: 60
Engine Displacement: 74 cubic inches
Engine Bore & Stroke: 3.44x3.97 inches
Weight: 783 pounds
Wheelbase: 60 inches
Wheel Size (F/R): 16/16 inches
Top Speed: 100 miles per hour
Number Produced: 5,300

Group. As the names suggest, this FLHFB dripped with options, among them front and rear chrome safety guards, luggage rack, windshield, passing lamps, and more.

But there was even more in store for Harley customers in the coming year, and by 1969, Harley-Davidson Motor Company had been acquired by American Machine and Foundry. A new era was about to unfold for America's premier motorcycle company.

Did You Know?

The Shovelhead engine, introduced in 1966, shares elemental design features with the original Sportster engine. Both motors have hemispherical combustion chambers to deliver more power than the engines they replaced.

To appreciate the 1971 FX Super Glide, it's best to go back a few years to 1963. That's when Harley-Davidson hired Willie G. Davidson—whose grandfather was one of the company's founding members—as a designer. By then, Willie G. was an experienced motorcyclist with an art background from the Art Center College of Design in Los Angeles, California. The combination led to the conception of the Super Glide, designed by Willie G. and considered America's first factory-built custom.

No doubt, the FX was groundbreaking for its time, packing the big kick of a Big Twin into a minimalist package. To accomplish this, Willie G. mounted a Sportster front end to an FLH frame. He also stripped the chassis of its familiar big bike garb, and the addition of the boat tail seat—introduced the previous year on the Sportster—further underscored the new model's sporty intentions.

The 1971 FX played a significant role in this author's professional career, too, for this was the bike on which I mastered the fine

art of drag racing. As a young staff editor for *Hot Bike* magazine in 1971, I was tutored by the late, great drag racer Leo Payne on how to properly launch a Big Twin off the line. My racing experience was with high-revving Japanese two-strokes, but Payne showed me how to make the best of any engine off the line. As a footnote, I blew up the FX's engine that day, but the knowledge I gained from Payne's tutorship remained with me ever since. I'll always respect Leo Payne, and I'll always have a soft spot in my heart for the 1971 FX Super Glide.

1971 MODEL FX SUPER GLIDE

Price: $2,230
Horsepower: 65
Engine Displacement: 74 cubic inches
Engine Bore & Stroke: 3.44x3.97 inches
Weight: 560 pounds
Wheelbase: 62 inches
Wheel Size (F/R): 19/16 inches
Top Speed: 110 miles per hour
Number Produced: 4,700

Did You Know?

The FX was a kick-start-only model. If you wanted to ride this sporty Big Twin, you needed to master the art of kicking over the engine. An electric starter found its way to the model in 1974, leading to the FXE.

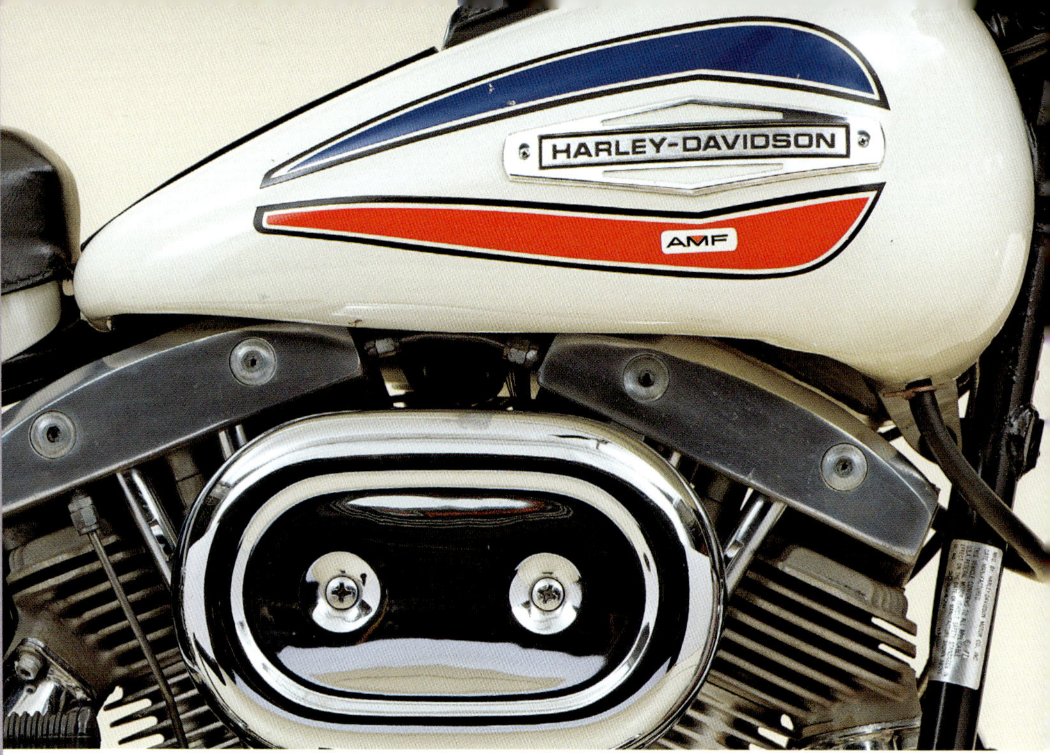
HARLEY-DAVIDSON
AMF

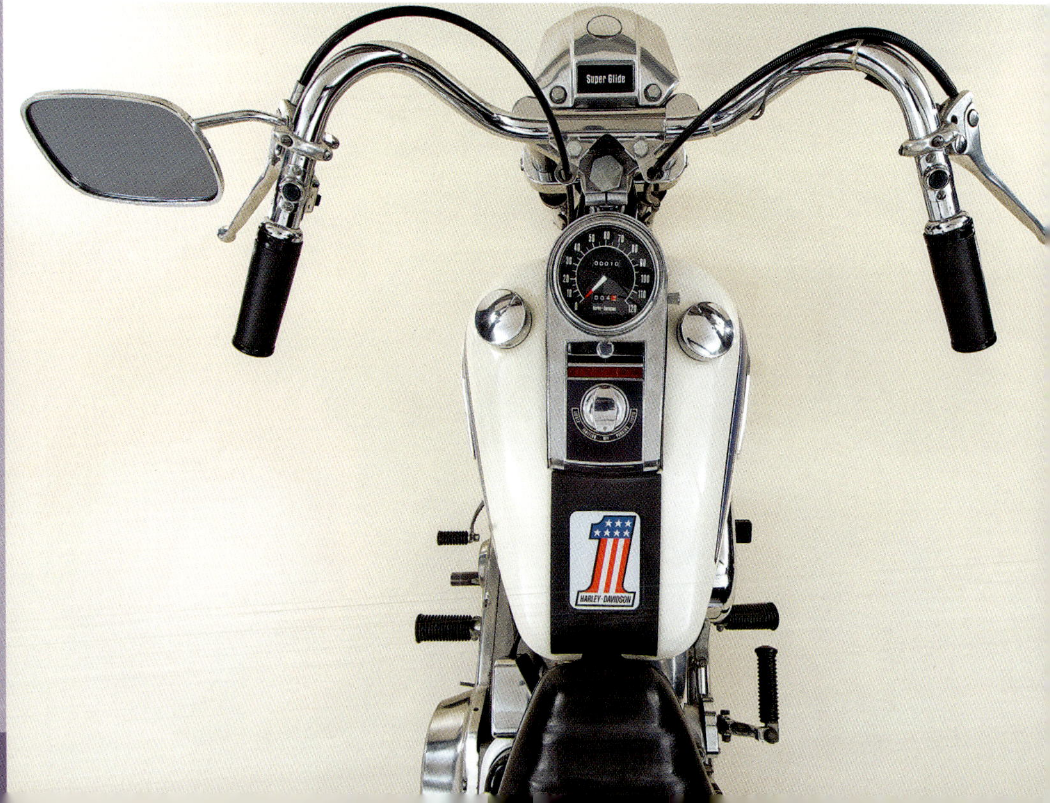
Super Glide

By 1973, the AMF/Harley-Davidson connection was in full swing, and by year's end most motorcycle assembly took place at the facility in York, Pennsylvania. That included Sportsters, which for 1973 were no longer called Sportsters! The 1973 model designation was simply XL-1000 (electric-start model) and XLCH-1000 (kick-start).

Displacement for the XL engine swelled to 1,000cc, or 61 cubic inches, in 1972 due to a larger cylinder bore size. The increased

1973 MODEL XL-1000

Price: NA
Horsepower: 61
Engine Displacement: 61 cubic inches
Engine Bore & Stroke: 3.19x3.81 inches
Weight: 492 pounds
Wheel Size (F/R): 19/18 inches
Quarter-mile Speed/ET: 97.7 miles per hour/13.38 seconds
Top Speed: 116 miles per hour
Number Produced: 9,875

bore required spacing the bolt pattern from the engine's centerline another 1/16 inch, so engine cases from 1971 to 1972 were no longer interchangeable. The troublesome Tillotson carburetor was also replaced in 1972. In its place, mixing fuel and air for the new 61-inch engine, sat a Bendix carburetor. "Unlike the Tillotson, the Bendix has a float bowl and an accelerator pump to improve gas metering," wrote the editors of *Hot Bike* magazine in the March 1972 issue.

The XL and XLCH also received a few new components for 1973. In a move to improve the ride and handling, a new front fork supplied by the Japanese vendor Showa was installed. The new front end also boasted a single hydraulic disc brake, a first for the XL line.

Did You Know?

Even though the Sportster's frame experienced several major changes for 1973, the most notable improvement was found up front. A new fork, built by Showa, sported a single disc brake.

1973 MODEL XL-1000

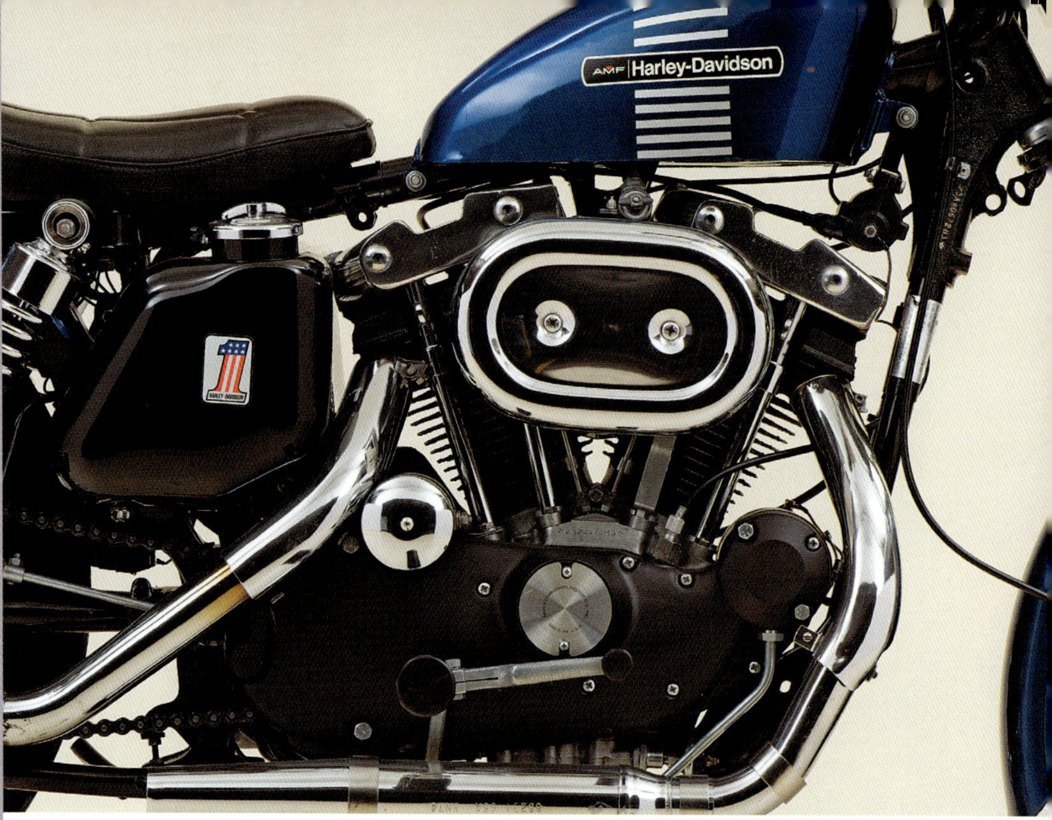

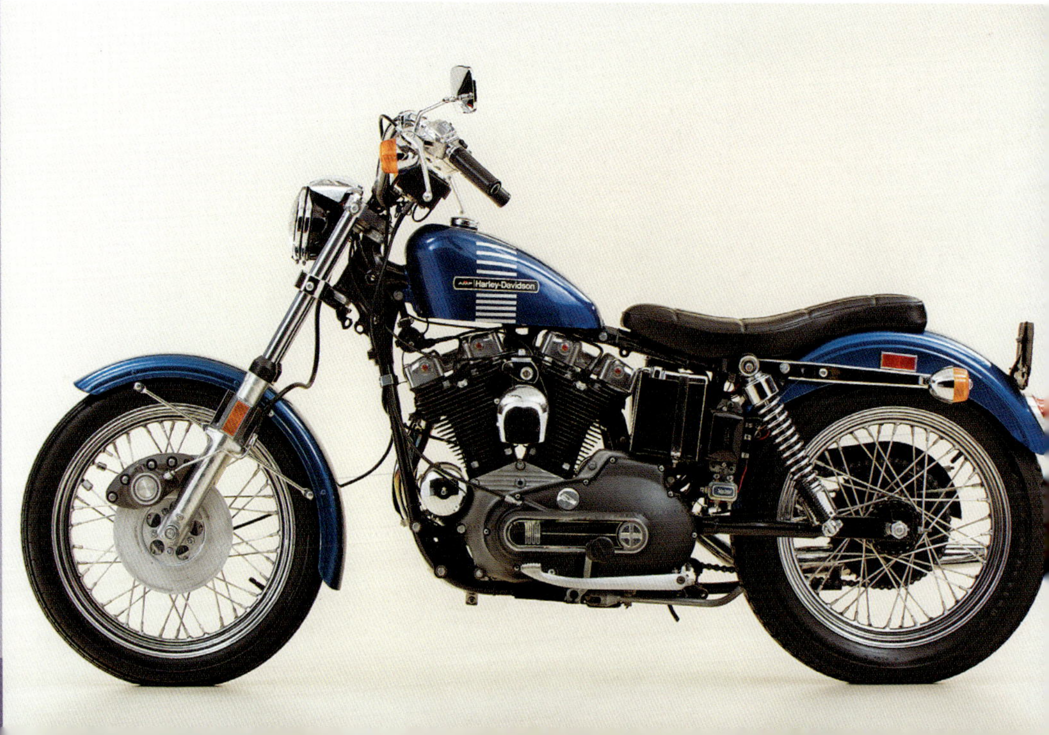

If it's true that idle hands lead to idle minds, then Russ Townsend's mind must have been at redline when he decided to give his 1973 FLH-1200 a fresh look. While recuperating from an accident, Russ decided to use his idle time to decorate the Electra-Glide that he and his wife, Margaret, owned with red, white, and blue rhinestones. One rhinestone led to another, and before you know it, the bike was, well, stoned. Russ estimates that he spent about $3,000 on the new family jewels.

And Russ didn't stop there. You'll find 200 lights placed on that big bagger, and other accessories include a low-profile seat, custom trunk, a citizen's band radio, and an S&S Cycle carburetor and air bell to feed the engine.

In terms of technical highlights for the model year, Harley-Davidson equipped the 1973 FLH with a rectangular swingarm, and behind those saddlebags rests another disc brake to complement the single disc up front that had been added to the model the previous year. While all that glitters is not gold, Harley-Davidson was clearly raising the standard for its long-distance model.

1973 MODEL FLH RHINESTONE

Price: $2,745

Horsepower: 65

Engine Displacement: 74 cubic inches

Weight: 722 pounds

Wheelbase: 61.5 inches

Wheel Size (F/R): 16/16 inches

Quarter-mile Speed/ET: 78.56 miles per hour/15.778 seconds

Top Speed: 99 miles per hour

Number Produced: 7,750

Did You Know?

In the March 1973 issue, *Supercycle* magazine's editors described an FLH test ride: "It is quite a feeling sitting on such a large hunk of machinery."

1973 MODEL FLH RHINESTONE

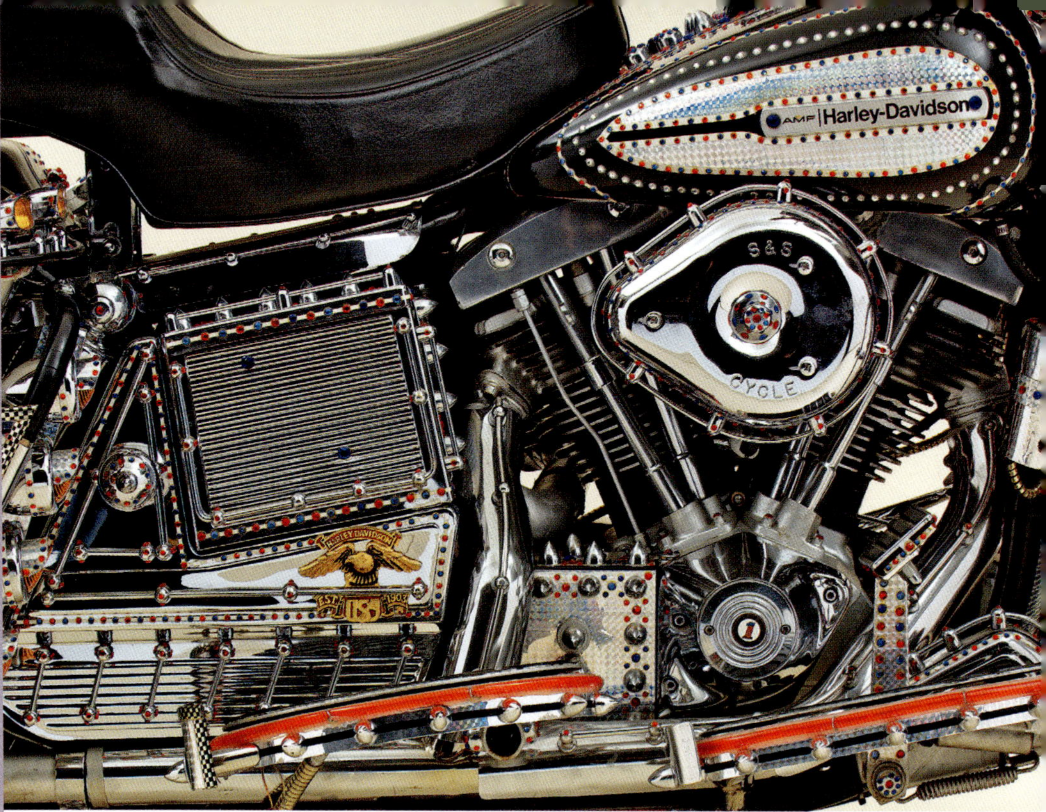

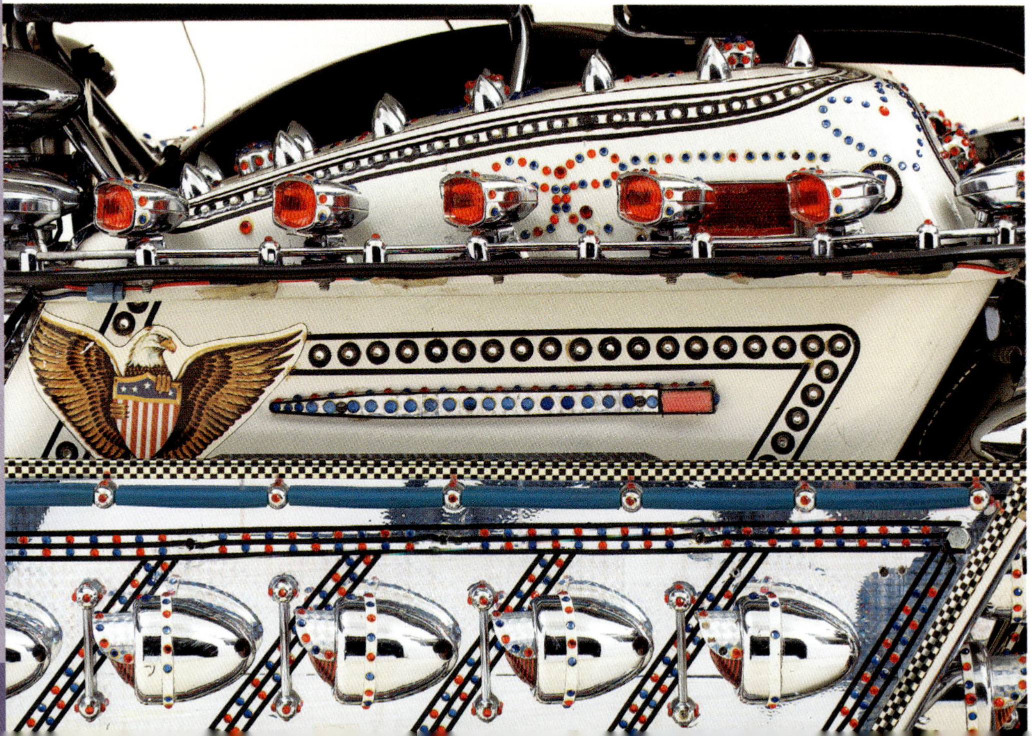

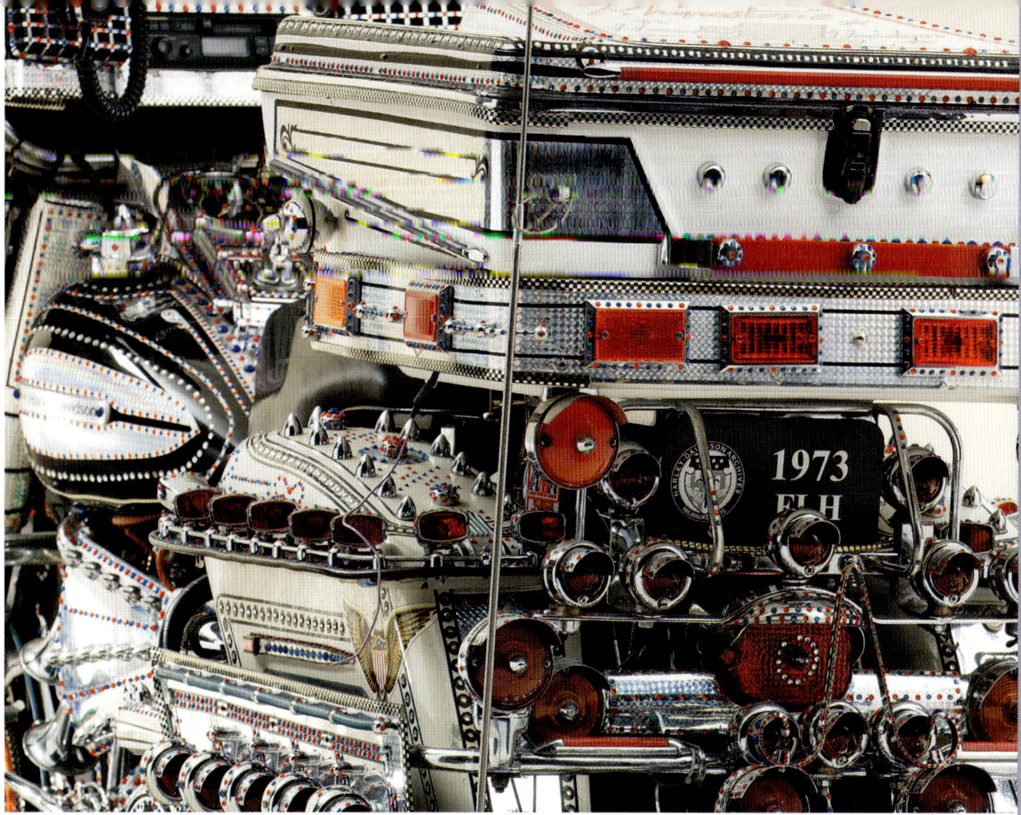
1973
FLH

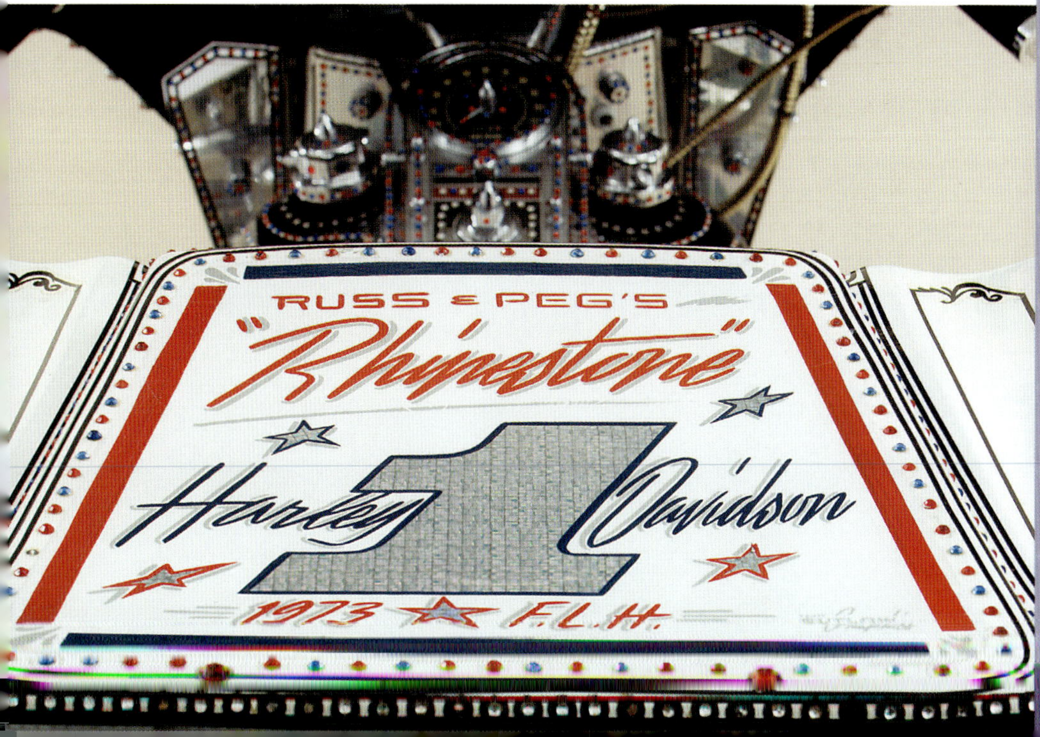
RUSS & PEG'S
"Rhinestone"
Harley 1 Davidson
1973 F.L.H.

While the 1977 XLCR Café Racer is best remembered for its European-inspired styling, perhaps the model's biggest contribution to future Harley designs was its brakes. This was the first Harley-Davidson to check in with three disc brakes—one on the swingarm and two on the fork. Later in the year, the FXS Low Rider also reported for duty wearing triple binders, and like its Café Racer sibling, the new custom Big Twin was a landmark design, for this was the bike that once and for all determined what an American sport cruiser would look like.

Despite the XLCR's radical styling penned by Willie G. Davidson, the all-black Café Racer wasn't a sales hit. In fact, more than a handful of the 1,923 XLCRs that were built didn't sell. An additional 1,201 units were manufactured the following year, and soon enough there was a surplus of the sporty model in dealers' showrooms across America. Many an XLCR found their way into a dealer's back room, where they sat for decades before Willie G.'s design became popular among collectors.

To the XLCR's credit, several of its design features influenced future models. Among those highlights were the XLCR's cast-aluminum wheels, dual front disc brakes, all-black cosmetics, and the frame's triangulated rear section, which was used on subsequent Sportsters and later on the FXR Big Twin that helped usher in the new Evolution V-2 engine in 1984.

1977 MODEL XLCR

Price: $3,595
Horsepower: 68
Engine Displacement: 61 cubic inches
Engine Bore & Stroke: 3.19x3.81 inches
Weight: 515 pounds
Wheelbase: 58.5 inches
Wheel Size (F/R): 19/18 inches
Top Speed: 110 miles per hour
Number Produced: 1,923

Did You Know?
The XLCR's iconic cast-aluminum wheels were from Morris and the disc brakes from Kelsey-Hayes. Allan Girdler wrote in his book, *Illustrated Harley-Davidson Buyer's Guide*, about the XLCR: "The XLCR didn't sell, either."

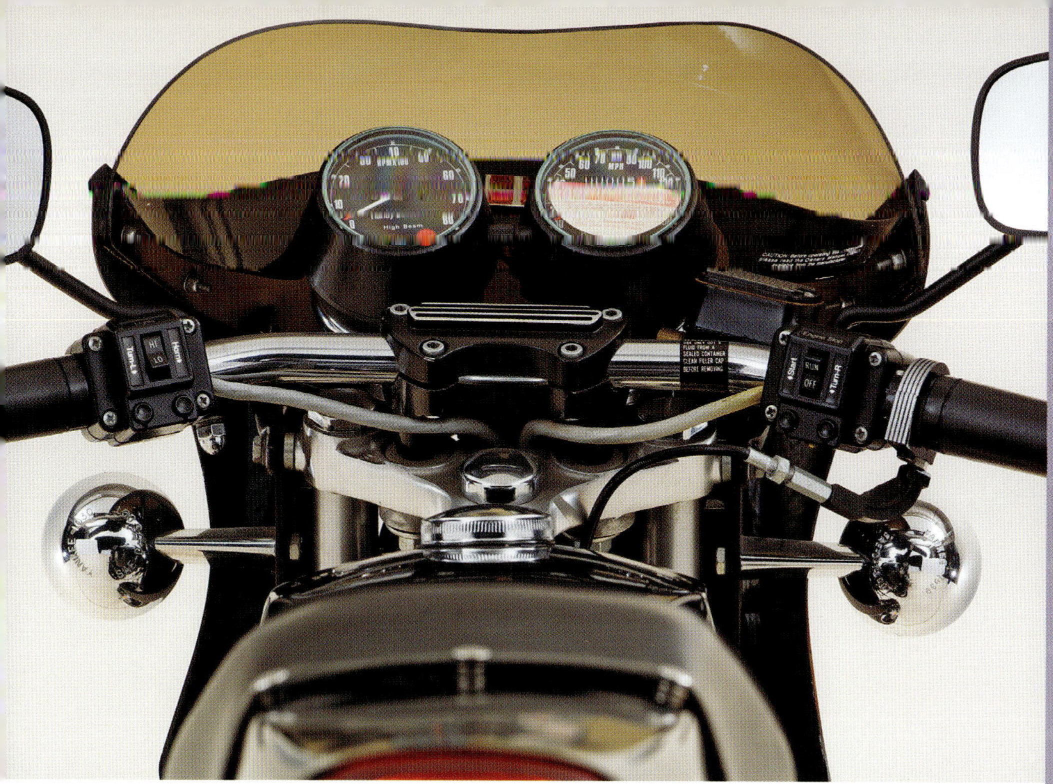
Horn
HI
LO
Turn-L
Start
RUN
OFF
Turn-R
High Beam

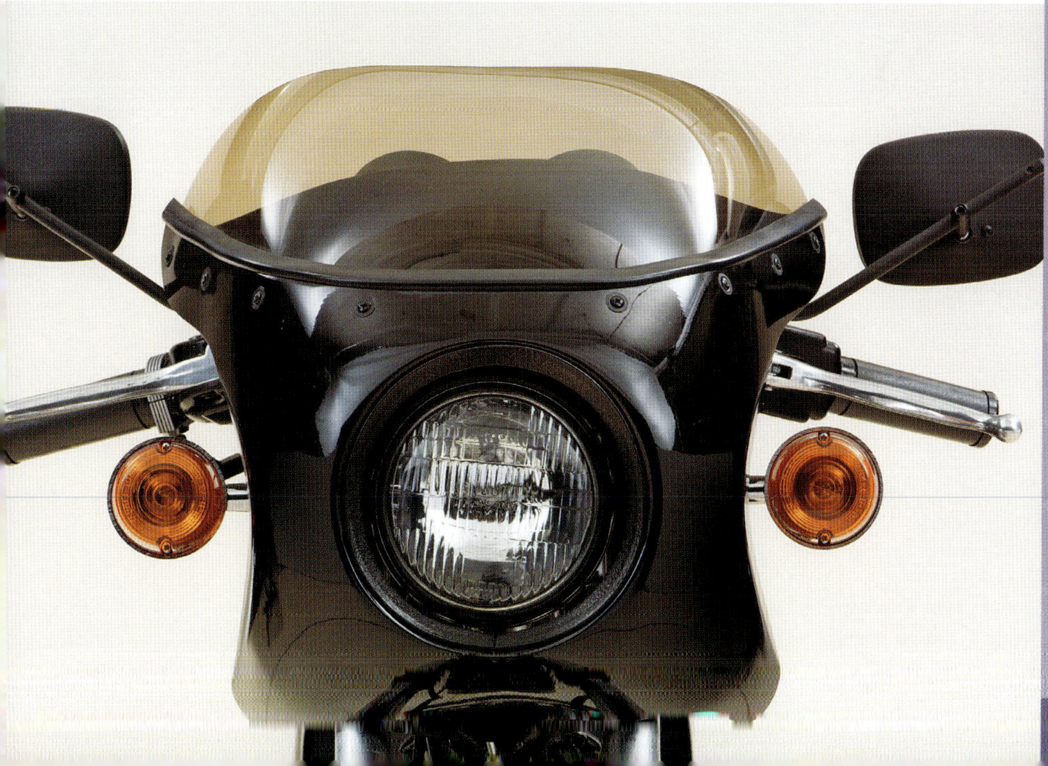

So what do you do when you've invested a lot of money and time into a model that doesn't sell well? Well, you take the favorable elements that went into that model, and you build on them. Such was the case with the XLH (electric start; the kick-start model was the XLCH), a model that picked up where the ill-fated XLCR left off in 1978.

Like the XLCR, the 1979 XLH cradled its 61-cubic-inch engine in a more rigid frame

that used a triangulated section to reinforce the critical rear motor mount/swingarm pivot section. Utilizing the tooling for the XLCR's signature Siamese exhaust system amortized costs for the XLH as well. Ditto

for the nine-spoke cast-aluminum wheels and dual front disc brakes.

Substitute the XLCR's unorthodox sheet metal with more conventional bodywork, paint it a bright color, add chromed and polished parts to the mix, and you have the XLH. It helped, too, that the engineers developed a more free-flowing air cleaner that improved intake flow by 10 percent and a new solid-state ignition to ensure stronger spark to the cylinders.

1979 MODEL XLH

Price: $3,610
Horsepower: 68
Engine Displacement: 61 cubic inches
Engine Bore & Stroke: 3.188x3.812 inches
Wheelbase: 58.5 inches
Wheel Size (F/R): 19/16 inches
Top Speed: 99 miles per hour
Number Produced: 6,525

Did You Know?
In addition to the new frame, the 1979 Sportster received a new rear master cylinder design. That same year, Harley-Davidson dropped the XLCR and XLT, replacing them with the XLS, which boasted an extended fork among other custom-bike features.

No offense to the kind folks of Sturgis, South Dakota, but they should rename their town Harleyville, or even Davidton. After all, every August without fail, the population of Sturgis swells from 5,500 to nearly half a million people who are there for the annual Black Hills Motorcycle Rally. And most of those seasonal residents ride their Harley-Davidson motorcycles to the event.

But, alas, it was Harley-Davidson that, in 1980, named a motorcycle after the town of Sturgis. The new model, the FXB-80 Sturgis, carried with it more than just a unique name. This was the bike that marked Harley's return to using belt drive. But reintroducing old technology wasn't a step back. In fact, the new belt marked a significant step forward. Within a few years, all Harley-Davidson motorcycles would use similar belt drives.

Harley engineers used the largest engine, the 80-cubic-inch Shovelhead, to power the Sturgis. It was the same motor that came on line in 1978 with the FLH. The following

year, the big Shovel could be found in the Fat Bob and FLHC Electra Glide Classic, and by 1980, the 80-incher was found in the Sturgis, Low Rider, Wide Glide, Electra Glide, and the new Tour Glide, which also used Harley's first five-speed transmission.

As for name changes, something was brewing in Milwaukee that would be reflected in how people addressed the Motor Company in the future. That change would involve 13 key members of the company's management team.

1980 MODEL FXB STURGIS

Price: NA
Engine Displacement: 80 cubic inches
Engine Bore & Stroke: 3.50x4.25 inches
Weight: 610 pounds
Wheelbase: 64.7 inches
Wheel Size (F/R): 19/16 inches
Seat Height: 27 inches
Top Speed: 106 miles per hour
Number Produced: 1,480

Did You Know?

The FXB Sturgis was the first modern belt-driven Harley-Davidson. This was the second model year for the FX line to use the 80-cubic-inch Big Twin engine introduced in 1978 with FLH-80.

1980 MODEL FXB STURGIS

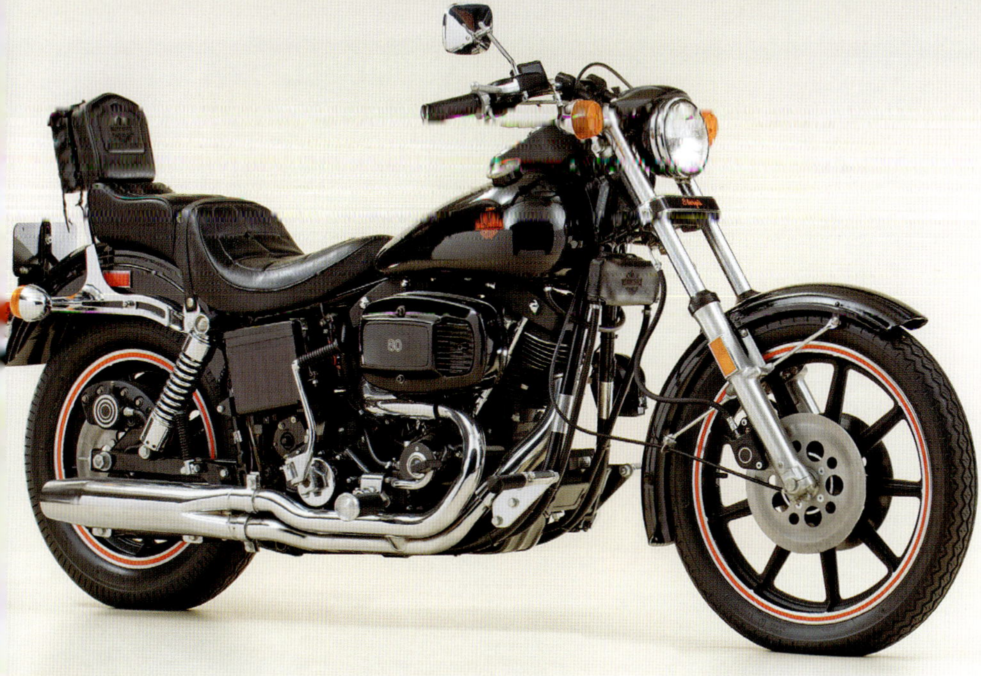

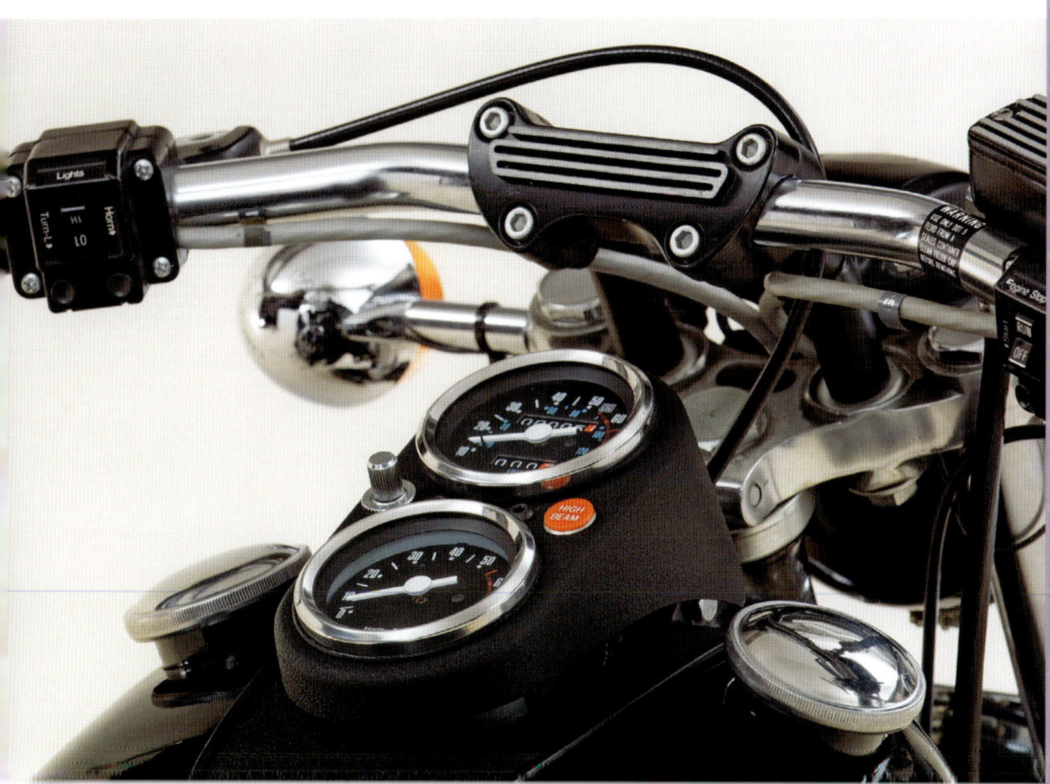

In June 1981, the Bar & Shield logo changed hands once again, as 13 members of Harley-Davidson's management team bought the company from American Machine and Foundry. Hardcore enthusiasts called the transaction a homecoming. Other people called it a long-shot gamble by the baker's dozen who had invested their fortunes into a floundering company.

But a savvy gambler knows when to hold and when to fold, and the new owners were holding some good cards, as history was

1982 MODEL FXRS SUPER GLIDE II

Price: $6,690
Engine Displacement: 80 cubic inches
Weight: 605 pounds
Wheelbase: 64.5 inches
Wheel Size (F/R): 19/16 inches
Seat Height: 28.7 inches
Quarter-mile Speed/ET: 93 miles per hour/13.92 seconds
Top Speed: 109 miles per hour
Number Produced: 3,190

about to prove. Their first ace in the hole was the FXRS Super Glide II, a bike that had an all-new frame that rode and handled like no other Harley-Davidson before. Turns out, too, that the new Super Glide II had panache. In the December 1981 issue of *Cycle Guide* magazine, the editors wrote of their FXRS road test: ". . . Harley-Davidson's new FXRS Super Glide II should erase all doubts: Americans still build the profilers with the most seductive presence on Main Street." Those few words made it known that

Harley-Davidson had just upped the ante in the cruiser-bike market.

The 3,190 FXRS customers got a motorcycle that had its 80-cubic-inch Shovelhead engine suspended in a rubber mount frame that was, in the words of the *Cycle Guide* report, "Good period." As it turned out, that good was about to get better, when the new Motor Company unveiled its new Evolution engine for 1984.

Did You Know?

The new reinforced FXR frame was nearly five times stiffer in torsion than the FX frame that it replaced. A rubberized engine-mounting system also considerably reduced vibration to the rider.

1982
FXRS

Two new Sportster models joined the lineup for 1983. One, the XLX, was considered a minimalist bike with a minimalist price of $3,995. To help keep costs down, the bike had a mild 883cc engine for power, a solo seat for the rider, and perched atop the frame's backbone was the familiar 2.2-gallon peanut gas tank.

The other Sportster was hell on wheels, a rip-roaring hot rod that made your blood boil and your driver's license cringe. We're talking about the XR-1000, and if you ever get the chance to ride one, do it. As a cross between an ordinary Sportster (the chassis and peanut gas tank) and a race-bred XR-750 (the engine, a 1,000cc V-twin fed by a pair of Dell'Orto slide-valve carburetors on the right side and race-signature upswept exhaust pipes on the left side), riding the XR-1000 was like experiencing a bar-room brawl every time the

traffic light turned green. The solid-mount motor snorted and roared, and the megaphone exhausts emitted a flatulent growl that would make any politically correct do-gooder blush. This was a motorcycle.

The first-year XR-1000 came in one color, Slate Grey, and sold for $6,995. Wienies need not apply for this bike—which is probably why Harley-Davidson introduced the XLX that same year.

1983 MODEL XR-1000

Price: $6,995
Horsepower: 70
Engine Displacement: 61 cubic inches
Weight: 470 pounds
Wheel Size (F/R): 19/16 inches
Quarter-mile ET: 12.88 seconds
Top Speed: 120 miles per hour
Number Produced: 1,018

Did You Know?

Many enthusiasts in 1983 described the XR-1000 as an exercise in engineering and marketing. Many of those same people claim that engineering won, which might help explain why the XR-1000 performed so poorly in sales. Simply, the bike needed a gas tank and seat that also resembled those found on the race-bred XR-750.

1983 MODEL XR-1000

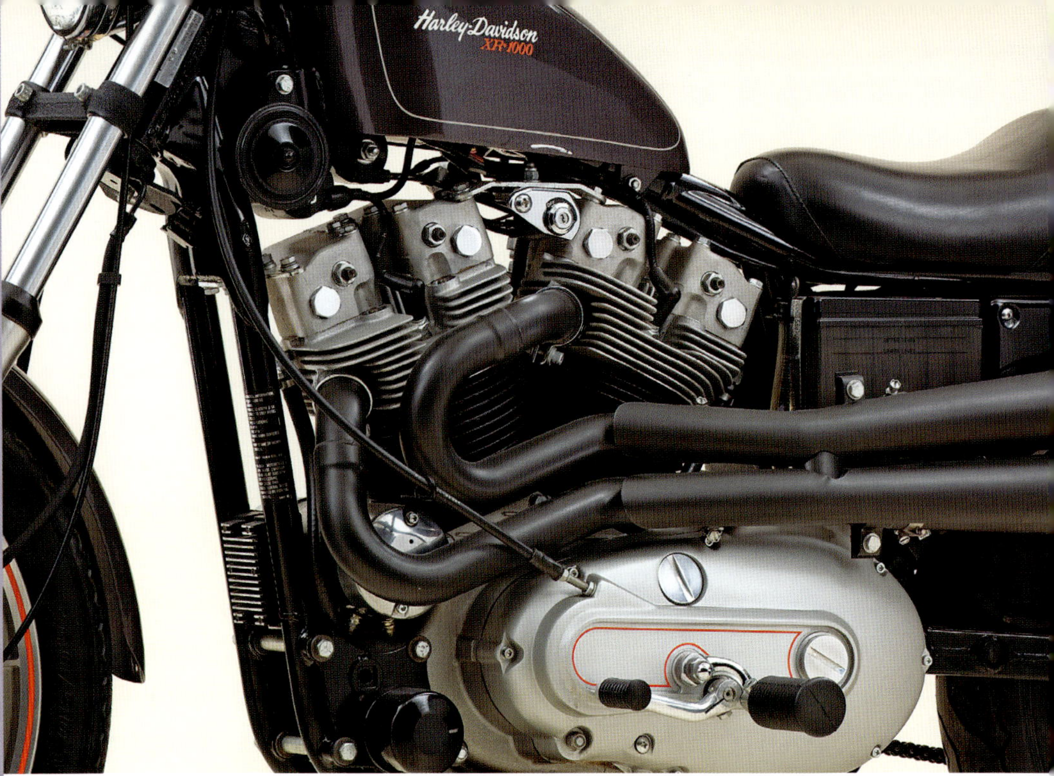

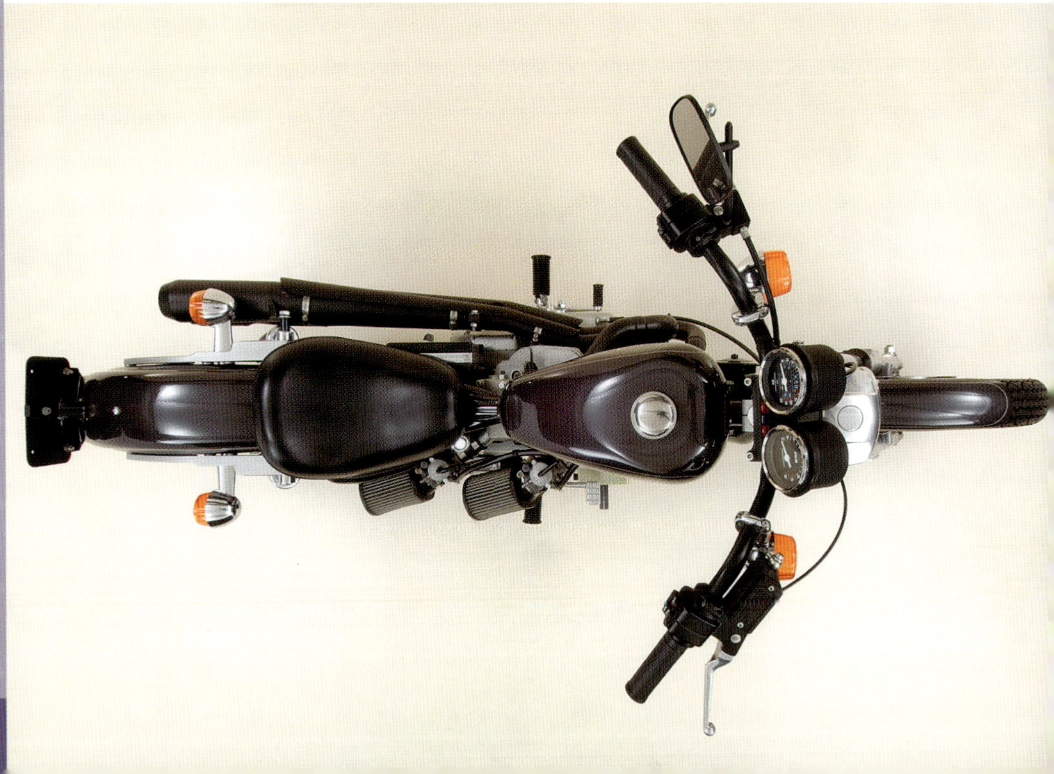

Belt-driven motorcycles were still somewhat of a novelty in 1983, and Harley-Davidson offered a couple new variations that utilized this maintenance-friendly system. Among those belt-drivers were the FXSB Low Rider and the new FXWG Wide Glide.

Perhaps the big news about the FXDG, though, was its rear disc wheel (thus the "DG" nomenclature for Disc Glide), the first of the new-breed Harleys with such a styling treatment. This theme, of course, would later become the focal point for the Fat Boy introduced in 1990.

1983 MODEL FXDG DISC GLIDE

Price: $7,699
Engine Displacement: 80 cubic inches
Weight: 585 pounds
Wheel Size (F/R): 21/16 inches
Number Produced: 810

The stubby, blacked-out exhaust was also evidence that Harley stylists were digging deeper into the Motor Company's bad-boy heritage to promote its products. They also looked to the past for the FXDG's monochromatic gas tank, emblazoned with a logo based on one used on 1919 models.

Clearly, the Motor Company's new owners were getting a better grip on what direction the company was headed. Their conclusion: Sales would sway heavily on the company's heritage and its connection with America's biker element.

Did You Know?

By 1983, many Harley-Davidson models were coming off the chain gang. Among those to use a belt final drive was the FXDG. Many FXDG owners often refer to this model as the "Willie G."

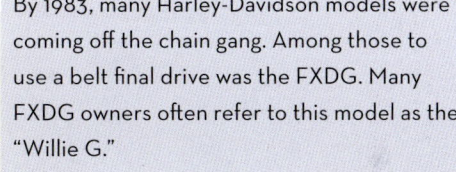

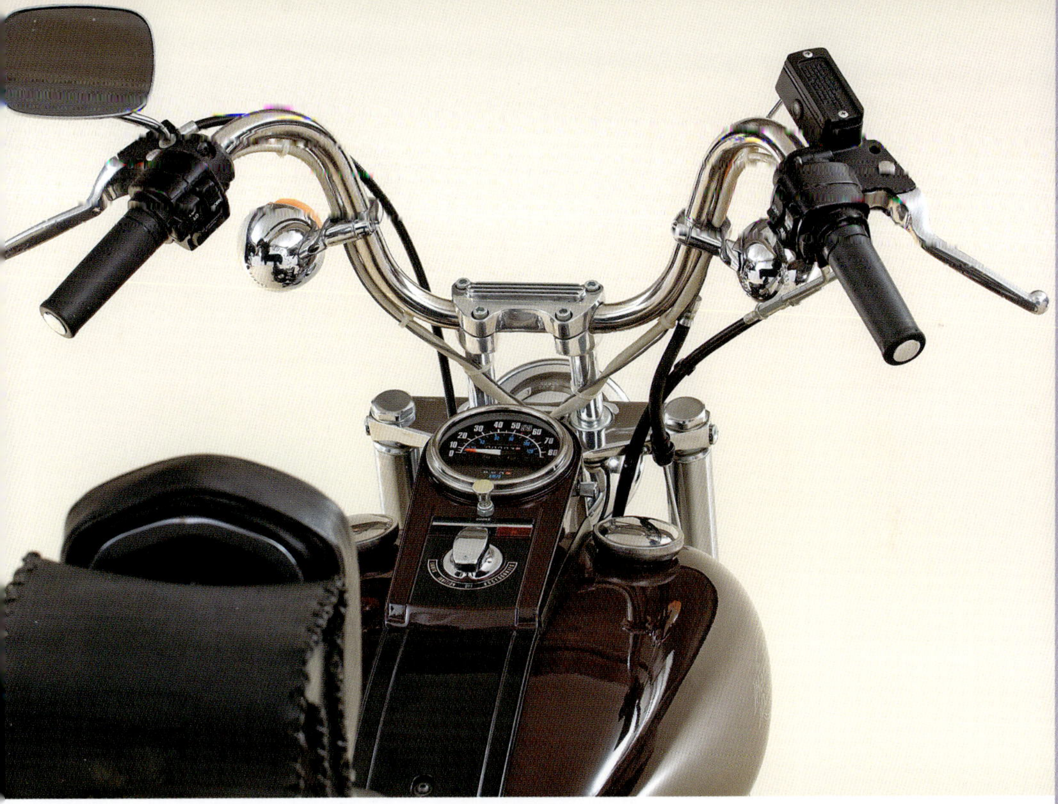

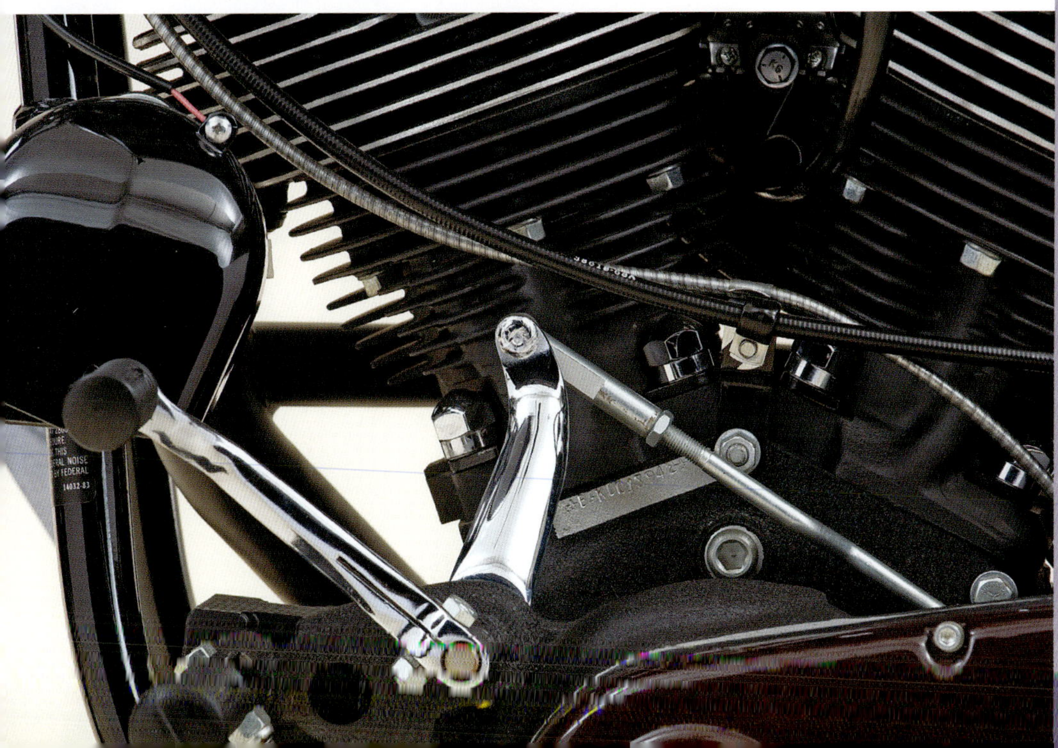

CHAPTER 5
INDEPENDENCE

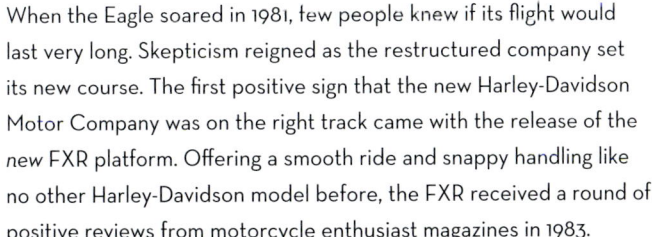

When the Eagle soared in 1981, few people knew if its flight would last very long. Skepticism reigned as the restructured company set its new course. The first positive sign that the new Harley-Davidson Motor Company was on the right track came with the release of the *new* FXR platform. Offering a smooth ride and snappy handling like no other Harley-Davidson model before, the FXR received a round of positive reviews from motorcycle enthusiast magazines in 1983.

For the following model year, Harley-Davidson dropped a bombshell with an all-new engine, and the explosion could be felt around the world. Nestled in the FXR chassis was a thoroughly modernized V-twin engine, called the Evolution V-2, a.k.a., the "Evo." New design features and current metallurgy made for a Big Twin engine that not only performed well, but was less prone to leaking oil, a malady common in many earlier designs.

1984 FXST

But there was more to come: The new Evo engine was shoehorned into a unique new frame design that evoked images of Harley-Davidson's golden bygone days, making the Softail a success even before the first one was sold. Practically overnight, Harley-Davidson dealers found themselves awash with customers wanting to buy the bike that had the nostalgic—and cool—looks of a rigid with the comfortable ride of a fully suspended chassis.

The Eagle was not only soaring, it was flying high! And in coming years it would continue to soar even higher.

The Harley-Davidson Motor Company redefined itself in 1984 with the FXST Softail. An all-new frame and engine bowed that year, and the face of the modern American biker changed forever. This is the model that offered the looks—mixed with a dash of heritage—found in the great American chopper. And it came packaged with the civility of a modern motorcycle.

The Softail name is derived from a frame that looked like a classic rigid frame. But hidden beneath the kick-start transmission were two shock absorbers that helped soften the ride via the triangulated swingarm that contributed to the FXST's old-time appearance. The Softail frame was actually based on a design by a couple of bike builders in St. Louis, Missouri. Harley-Davidson bought rights to their frame, developed it to its potential, and in 1984 rocked the cruiser bike world with the FXST.

Further change—evolution, if you will—was found in the engine. The FXST is the model that best showcased the new Evolution (or Evo) V-2 engine that bowed in 1984. This 80-cubic-inch engine incorporated newer, lighter-weight material than found on previous Big Twins, which contributed to a tighter engine that was less prone to oil leakage. It helped, too, that the Evo produced more power than its predecessors.

1984 MODEL FXST SOFTAIL

Price: $7,999
Engine Displacement: 80 cubic inches
Engine Bore & Stroke: 3.50x4.25 inches
Weight: 628 pounds
Wheelbase: 66.3 inches
Wheel Size (F/R): 21/16 inches
Top Speed: 110 miles per hour
Number Produced: 5,413

Did You Know?

It can be argued that the FXST was the model that saved Harley-Davidson. The all-new model boasted features—the new Evolution engine, a retro-styled Softail frame, and belt final drive, to name a few—that would prove popular for the coming years.

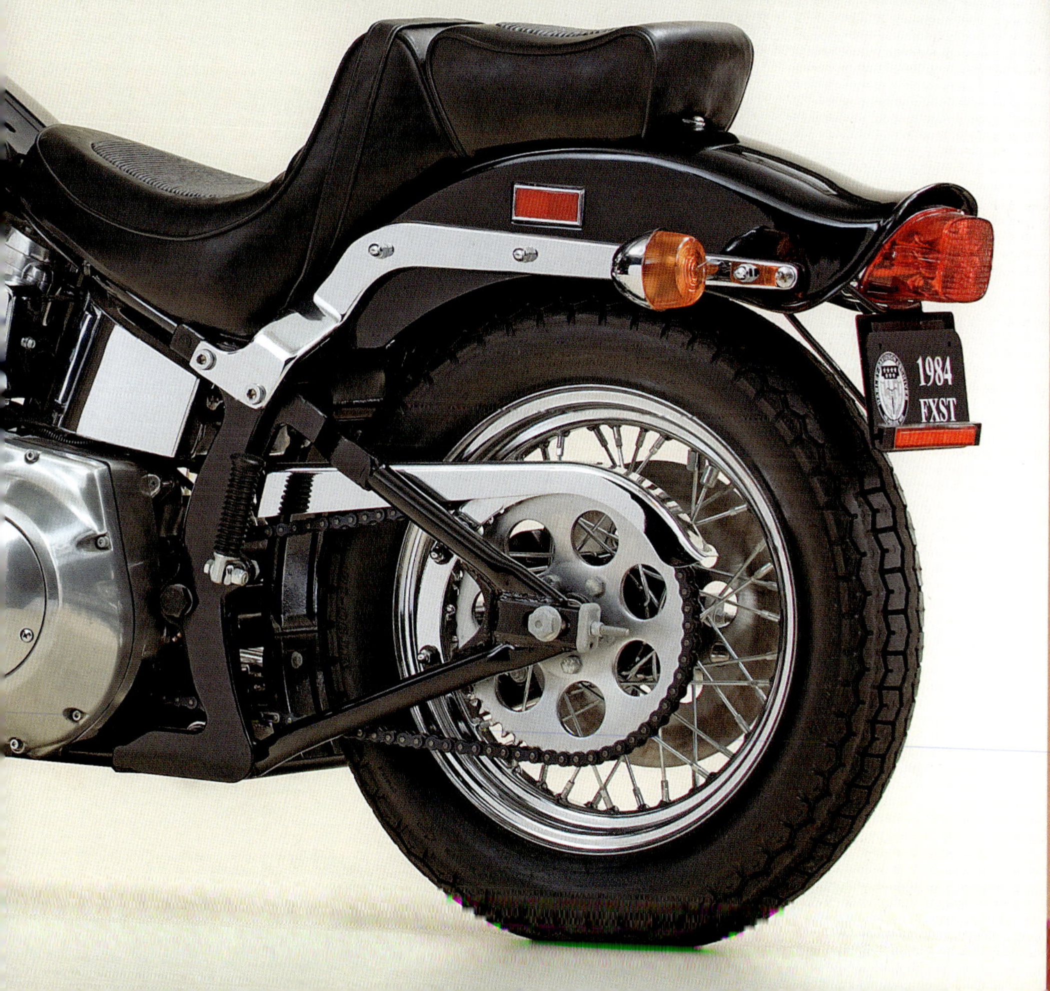

1984
FXST

Many motorcycle historians credit 1984, the year that Harley-Davidson bolted its new Evolution engine into an equally new Softail frame, as the turning point for the Motor Company's return to prominence. If so, then 1990 ranks as the year in which Harley-Davidson established itself once and for all as the brand that all other motorcycle companies would follow in the world of cruisers. And leading the way was Harley's new Fat Boy, a model that's been described as elegant, cutting edge and, well, *fat*.

Here's what the editors at *Cycle World* had to say in their January 1990 road test: "What's different is the Fat Boy's

1990 FAT BOY

Price: $11,115
Horsepower: 55
Engine Displacement: 80 cubic inches
Weight: 665 pounds
Wheelbase: 62.5 inches
Wheel Size (F/R): 16/16 inches
Tire Size (F/R): MT60-16
Seat Height: 26.5 inches
Quarter-mile Speed/ET: 91.46 miles per hour/14.53 seconds
Top Speed: 112 miles per hour
Number Produced: 4,440

monochromatic paint and beefier styling, making it seemingly more solid than any other machine in the H-D lineup."

In truth, the Fat Boy model represents more than just aggressive styling. This is the model that ushered in a redesigned clutch diaphragm spring to reduce lever pull. Also debuting on the Fat Boy engine was a new constant-velocity CV Keihin 40mm carburetor, producing more precise throttle response across the rpm range.

But it was *Cycle World*'s closing statement in the 1990 road test that proved most prophetic: "Combining retro-styling with the latest in Harley technological soundness, the Fat Boy shows the potential to become a key player in continuance of the Harley-Davidson legend." How true that proved to be.

Did You Know?

When the Fat Boy was introduced in 1990, nearly 57 percent of Softail buyers owned or had owned a Harley-Davidson motorcycle.

1990 FAT BOY

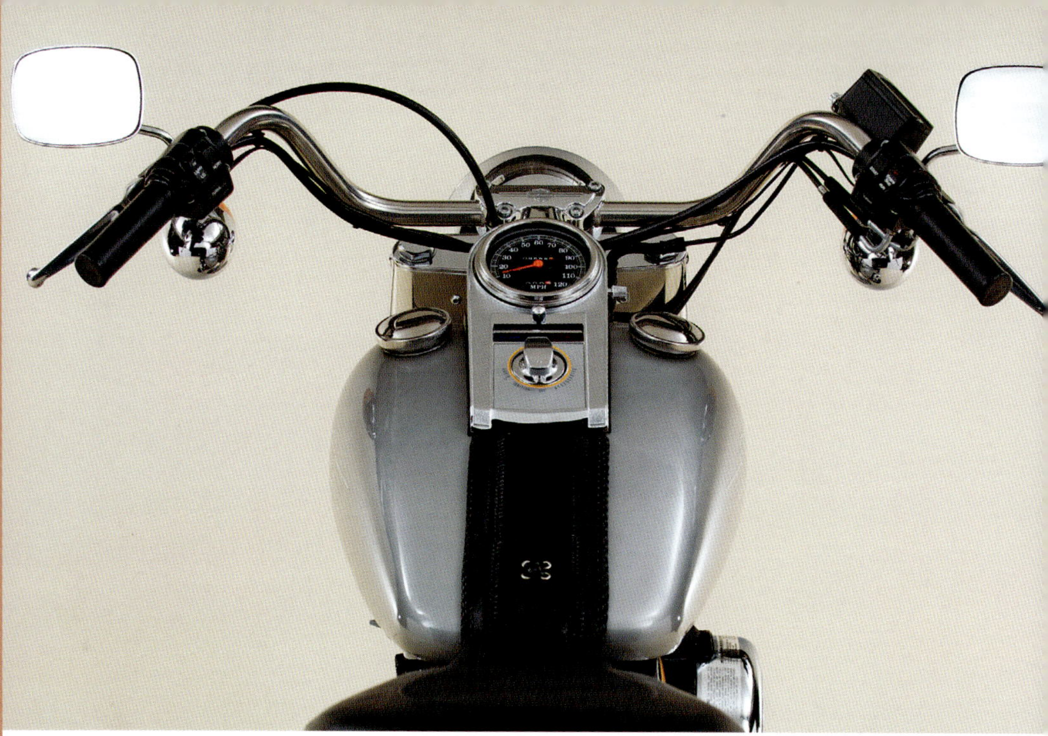

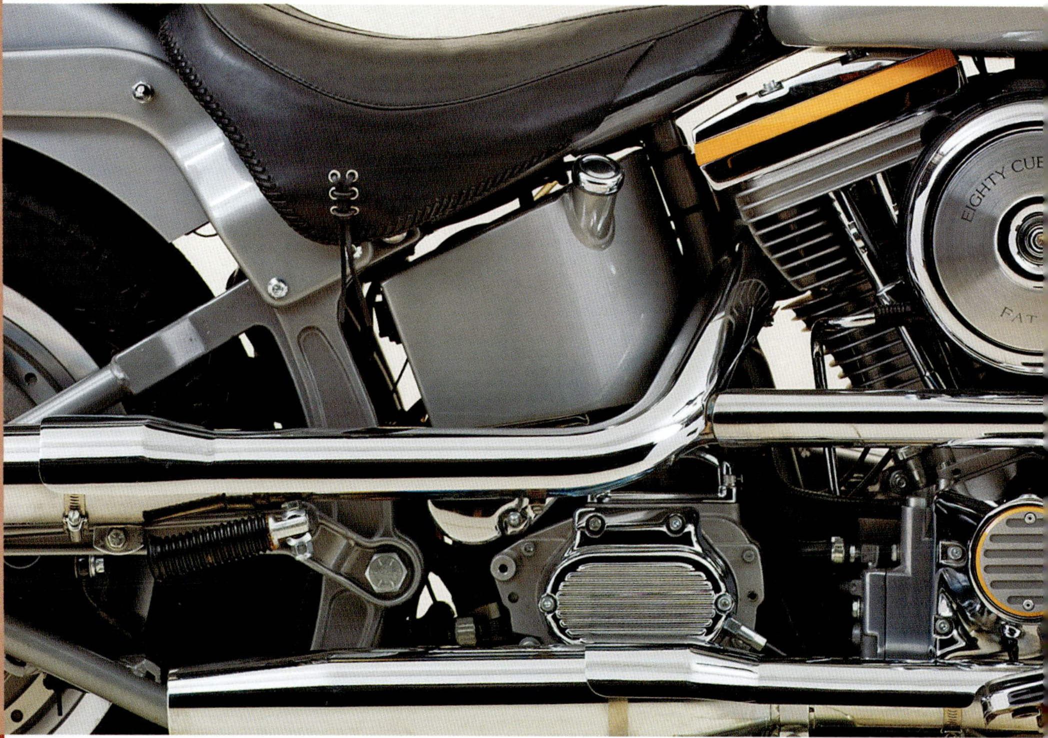

1990
FLSTF

When the late Wyatt Fuller opened the doors to Razorback Cycles in March 1993, his main goal was to help create new and exciting custom parts for Harley-Davidson. So when the Motor Company's clothing and apparel division wanted to promote its new line of denim jeans for Harley riders, it commissioned Fuller's shop to build a bike that played on the theme. What Fuller rolled out of his shop was an FLSTN customized

1994 MODEL FLSTN FAT BOY
BIKER BLUES

Price: NA
Engine Displacement: 80 cubic inches
Weight: 650 pounds
Wheelbase: 63.9 inches
Wheel Size (F/R): 16/16 inches
Seat Height: 26.5 inches
Number Produced: NA

to look like a Fat Boy and wrapped in that distinctive American fabric.

The secret to *Biker Blues* was in the paint Fuller's brush strokes left the look of blue denim on the Fat Boy's sheet metal. There was plenty of art in the detail, too, and the paint scheme looked as if it had zippers, seams, and rivets, even worn spots.

The trained eye noticed some custom-made parts on the bike as well. The rear fender struts, floorboards, chin spoiler beneath the engine, air cleaner, clutch and primary access covers, and final drive pulley, to name a few parts, were fabricated by Fuller.

As for the biker denim jeans, Harley-Davidson claimed in promotional material that they were "the only jeans with the Harley-Davidson pedigree. They're made from heavy 14 1/2-oz. cotton denim to be rough, rugged and ready to ride."

Did You Know?

There are essentially two classes of Softails. Those with the FX designation have 21-inch front wheels; the FL series, such as the Fat Boy, wrap their front rubber around 16-inch wheels.

"The most conservative motorcycle company in the world—that would be Harley-Davidson—just kicked the rest of the motorcycle establishment right smack in the groin." So wrote the editors of *IronWorks* magazine in the October 2001 issue when introducing the revolutionary V-Rod.

What's a V-Rod? The *IronWorks* editors explain: "It's a model that spearheads a whole new platform by Harley-Davidson, called the VRSC, which in Milwaukee lingo stands for 'V-twin, Racing, Street, Custom.'"

2002 MODEL VRSCA V-ROD

Price: $16,995
Horsepower: 115
Engine Displacement: 69 cubic inches (1,130cc)
Engine Bore & Stroke: 3.94x2.83 inches
Weight: 615 pounds
Wheelbase: 67.5 inches
Wheel Size (F/R): 19/18 inches
Quarter-mile Speed/ET: 116.91 miles per hour/11.53 seconds
Top Speed: 137 miles per hour
Number Produced: NA

Indeed, the V-Rod was an all-new platform, its Revolution engine representing the first liquid-cooled model to bear the famous Bar & Shield logo. The 1,130cc (69 cubic inches) engine's cylinders have a 60-degree spread. The dual-overhead-cam (DOHC) engine houses four valves per cylinder, and compression ratio checks in at 11.3:1. The 2002 Revolution produced 115 horsepower at the crankshaft, and torque was rated at a generous 74 lb-ft at 7,000 rpm. Redline was set at 9,000 rpm. "The engine represents the centerpiece jewel for the bike," stated Willie G. Davidson, who had a significant role in the bike's genesis.

Other "revolutionary" technology could be found in the hydro-formed aluminum frame, shrouded radiator, and raw aluminum finish. The V-Rod clearly showed the world that Harley-Davidson was capable of producing more than just low-riding cruisers and baggers. The Revolution was on.

Did You Know?

The V-Rod won a four-bike shootout in the March 2002 issue of *Cycle World* in which the editors stated: "The V-Rod wins not only for what it is here and now, which is a genuinely gorgeous hot-rod cruiser that accelerates like a superbike and profiles like a showbike, but also wins for what it portends in the power-cruiser class: More motorcycles with character, style, and real performance."

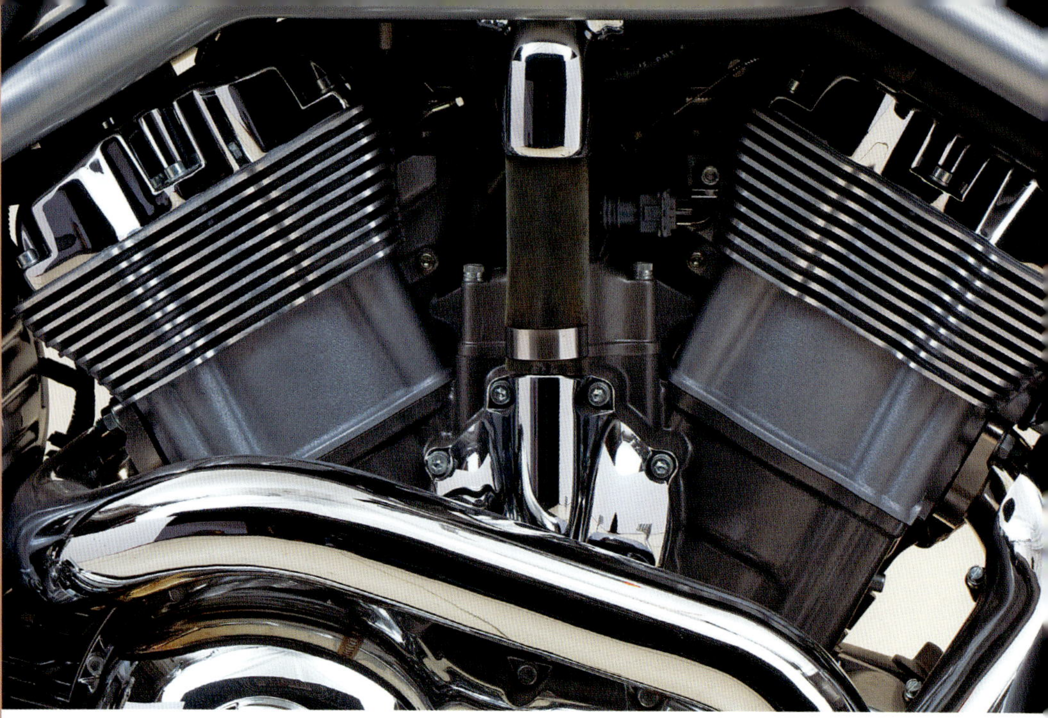

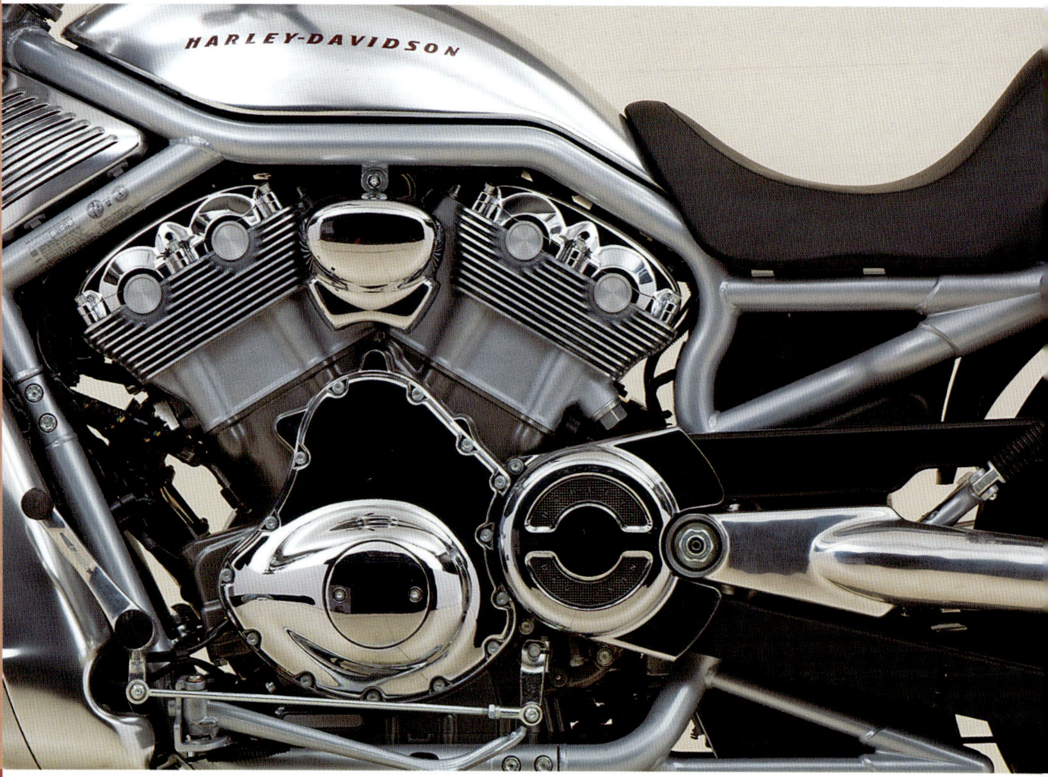
HARLEY-DAVIDSON

2002 MODEL VRSCA V-ROD

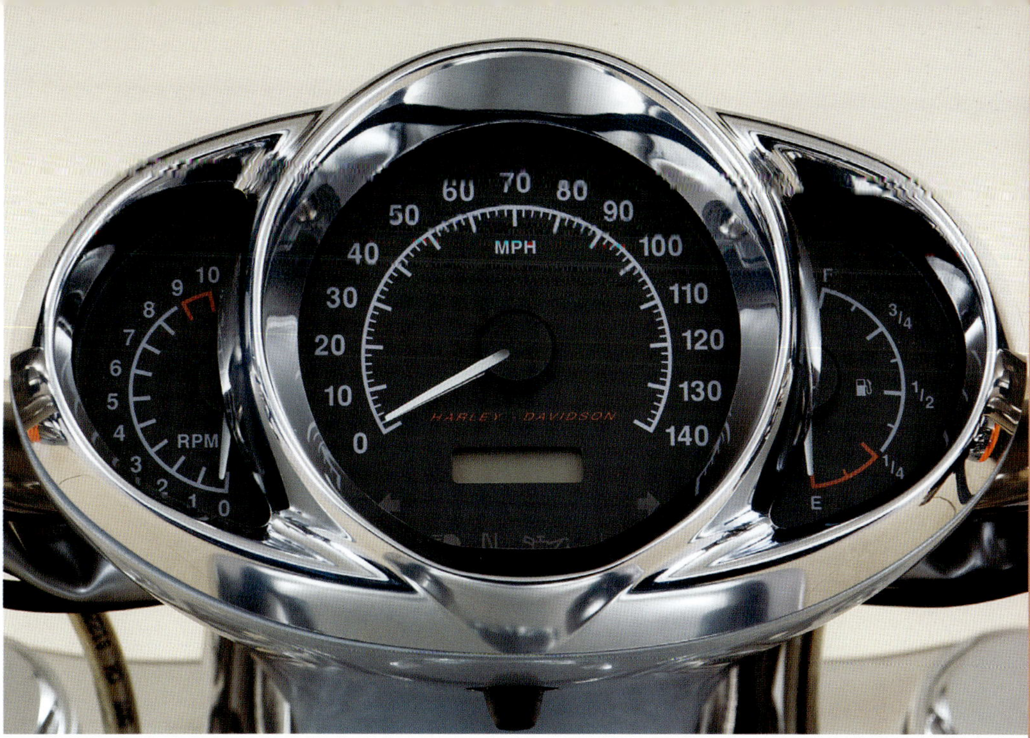

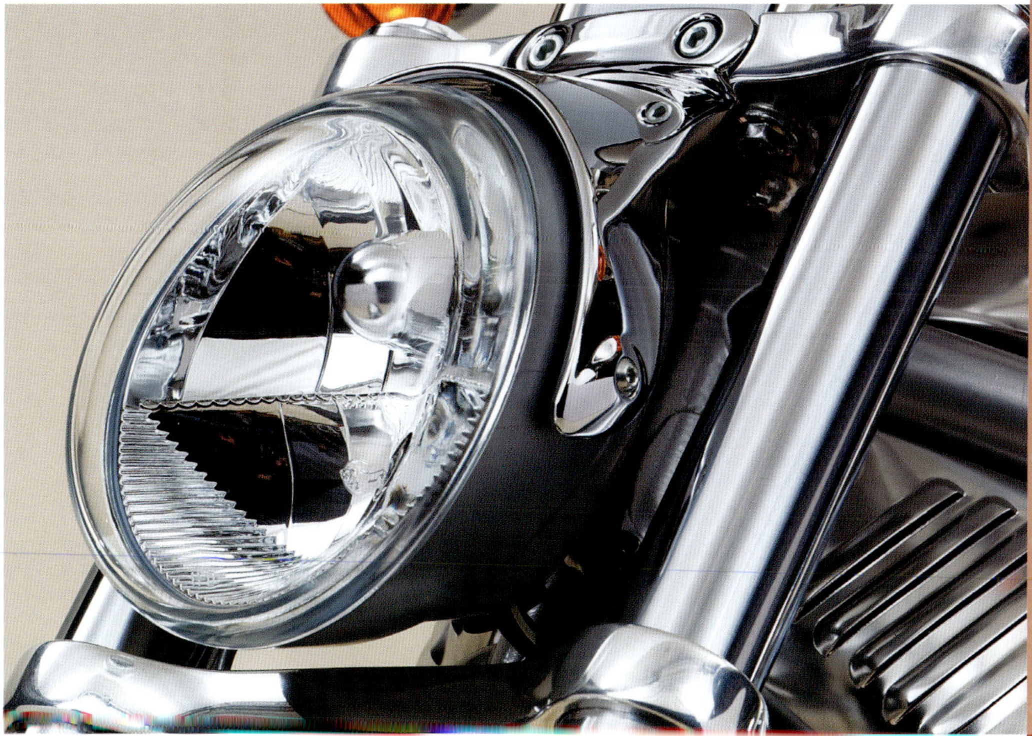

If you were to walk into a Harley-Davidson dealership in 2004 to order an Electra-Glide Classic and you checked every box under "model upgrades," your bike still wouldn't have all the features found on a Screamin' Eagle Electra-Glide from the Custom Vehicle Operations (CVO) division. Fact is, all CVO models—and every year Harley-Davidson generally offers four—have more accessories than what's available for their standard-issue counterparts. In the case of the Screamin'

2004 CVO ELECTRA-GLIDE

Price: $28,595
Torque: 100 lb-ft at 3,500 rpm
Engine Displacement: 103 cubic inches
Engine Bore & Stroke: 3.875x4.375 inches
Weight: 785 pounds
Wheelbase: 63.5 inches
Wheel Size (F/R): 16/16 inches
Tire Size (F/R): MT90-16/MT85-16
Seat Height: 26.5 inches
Number Produced: 2,500

Eagle Electra-Glide, the add-on list included more than 60 items ranging from handy, easy-to-pack saddlebag liners to the earth-shaking, 103-cubic-inch engine that produced more than 100 horsepower and an equal number of foot-pounds of torque. As the editors from *Hot Bike* explained in their June 2004 issue, the upgrades included "enough stuff to justify its $28,595 calling card."

But just because you placed an order for a Screamin' Eagle bagger didn't guarantee that you'd take delivery. As Harley does with all CVO models, only a limited number of these 785-pound bikes were available. In all, about 2,500 Screamin' Eagle baggers were produced for the year. The limit, it seems, was on the number of bikes sold, not on the bike itself.

Did You Know?

This marked the first year that Harley-Davidson's premier touring model received the Screamin' Eagle treatment that included the 103-cubic-inch engine. *American Rider* magazine added in its road test: ". . . the need for speed and power is certainly satisfied with the SE's big 103-inch engine."

2004 CVO ELECTRA-GLIDE

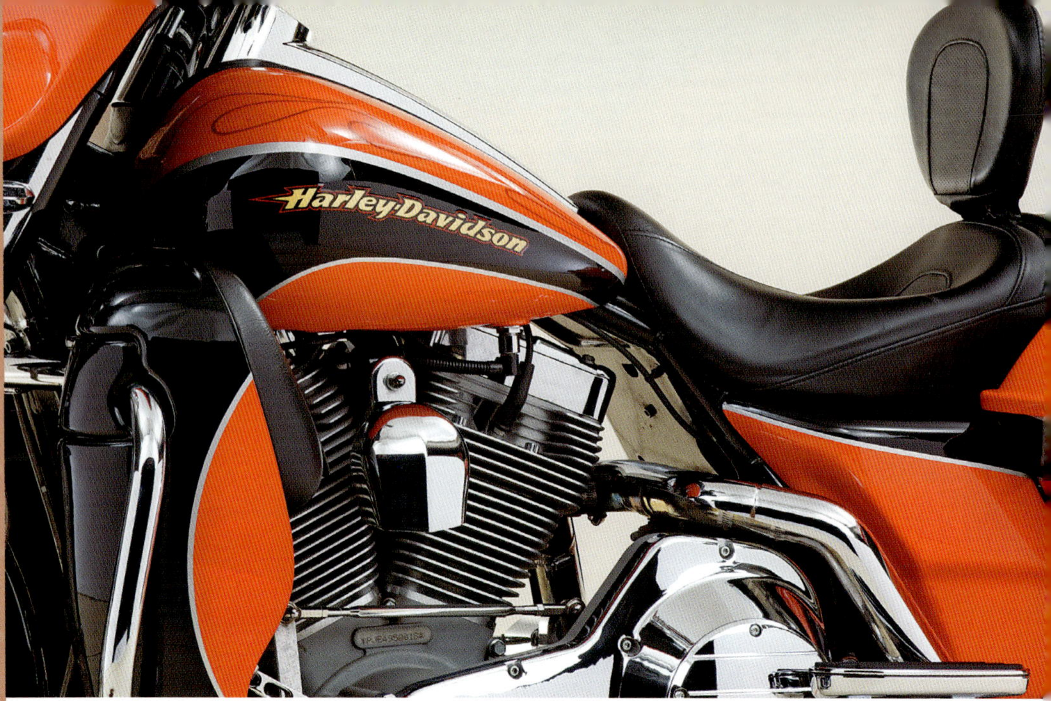

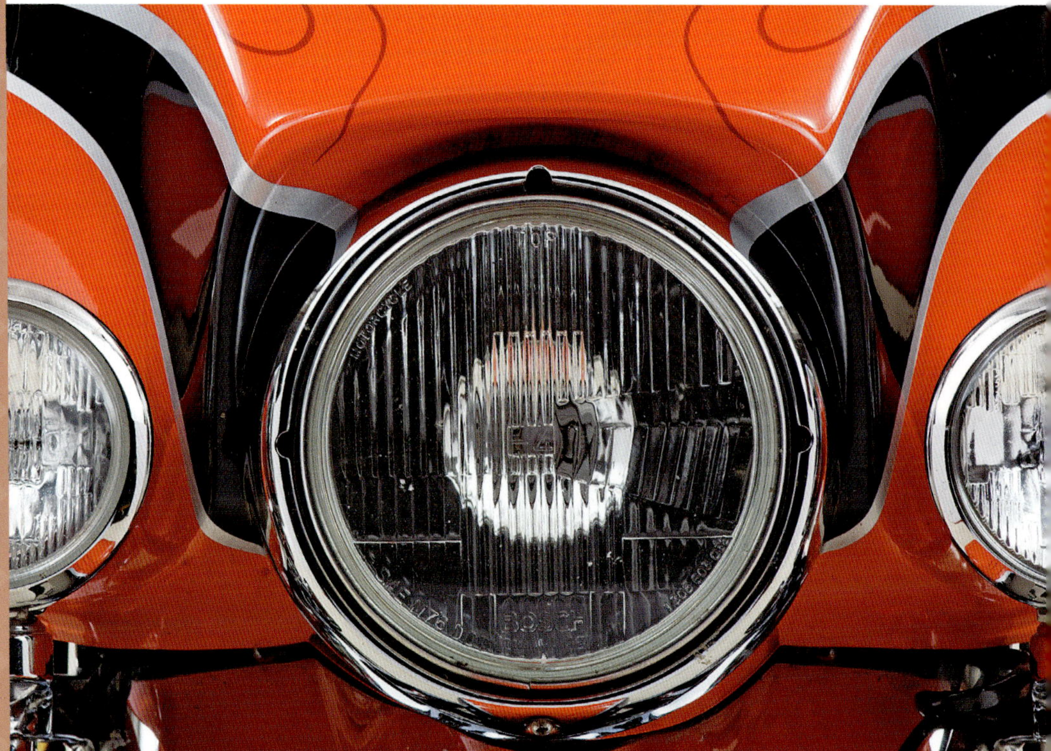

As Harley-Davidson enters its next 100 years of building motorcycles, it does so with one eye on tradition, the other focused squarely on the future. And a good example of that philosophy is the XL 1200N Sportster Nightster. A member of what Harley-Davidson's marketing department dubbed the Dark Customs, the Nightster is hip and cool, yet legal and user-friendly. Need proof? Here's what Chris Maida, editor for *American Iron* magazine, had to say in his July 2007 report:

"The bottom line is, though the Nightster is basically the same as other 2007 1200cc Sportsters, the bike's more aggressive pit bull/bad-boy look definitely sets it apart from its more conservative brothers in both styling and ride. I've been toolin' around on Sportsters for over three decades, and the XL 1200N made me think of some of the 1960s and '70s vintage Ironheads I rode back in the day. I had a lot of fun on those cantankerous machines and got the tickets to prove it. (Thankfully, the XL 1200N handles and runs a lot better!)"

The Nightster owes much of its bold image to a young Harley-Davidson stylist, 27-year-old Richard Christoph, who was assigned to give the Nightster its bad-boy look. The Nightster should help the Motor Company blaze its new path for years to come.

2007 MODEL XL 1200N SPORTSTER NIGHTSTER

Price: $9,595
Torque: 79.1 lb-ft at 4,000 rpm
Engine Displacement: 1,200cc
Weight: 565 pounds
Wheelbase: 60 inches
Wheel Size (F/R): 19/16 inches
Seat Height: 25.3 inches
Number Produced: NA

Did You Know?

The XL 1200N Nightster was introduced midyear, after the rest of the 2007 models were announced. It joined an elite group of bikes in the lineup that constitute what the Motor Company calls Dark Customs.

Harley-Davidson acknowledged the revolutionary nature of its liquid-cooled V-Rod in the name of the bike's engine: the Revolution. Since a revolution consists of more than one shot, it only made sense for the Motor Company to follow up with more V-Rod models, the most radical of which is the V-Rod Muscle.

Over the years the V-Rod engine has grown in displacement from 1130cc to 1250cc, thanks to an increase in bore to 4.13 inches. In V-Rod Muscle form, the 1250cc Revolution Twin engine benefits from the additional breathing conferred by the satin-chrome straight-shot side pipes, making the Muscle crank out 86 lb-ft of

torque. The potent engine generates an honest 105 horsepower at the rear wheel, meaning crankshaft horsepower is north of 120 ponies. With power like that, the Muscle's engine doesn't so much propel the motorcycle as it twists the earth backwards underneath its fat 240mm-wide rear tire.

It wouldn't do for Harley to dress a motorcycle this extraordinary in ordinary body work. From the low-profile rear fender that looks shrink-wrapped around the fat rear tire to the front sport fender with color-matched bracing, the Muscle doesn't look like any other bike in Harley's lineup. Like the iconic American muscle cars with which it shares its name, the Muscle even has a pair of scoops flanking its "fuel tank" (which is in reality a cover for the airbox; the real 5-gallon fuel tank is located under the seat).

The era of the classic muscle car may be long gone, but with the V-Rod Muscle Harley-Davidson has made certain that fans of two-wheeled muscle have not had to kick their high-performance habits.

2009 MODEL VRSCF V-ROD MUSCLE

Price: $17,199
Horsepower: 115
Engine Displacement: 76.28 cubic inches (1250cc)
Engine Bore & Stroke: 4.13 x 2.83 inches
Weight: 640 pounds
Wheelbase: 67 inches
Wheel Size (F/R): 19/18 inches
Number produced: NA

Did You Know?
The airbox cover and air-intake vents of the V-Rod Muscle were revised for the 2010 model year.

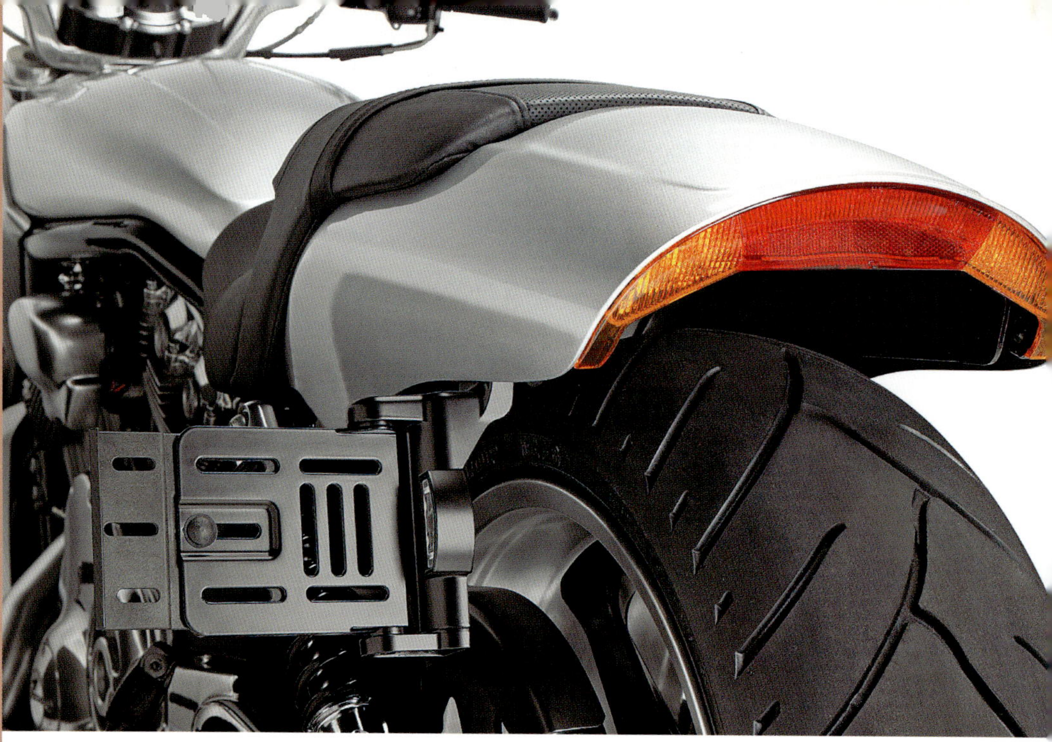

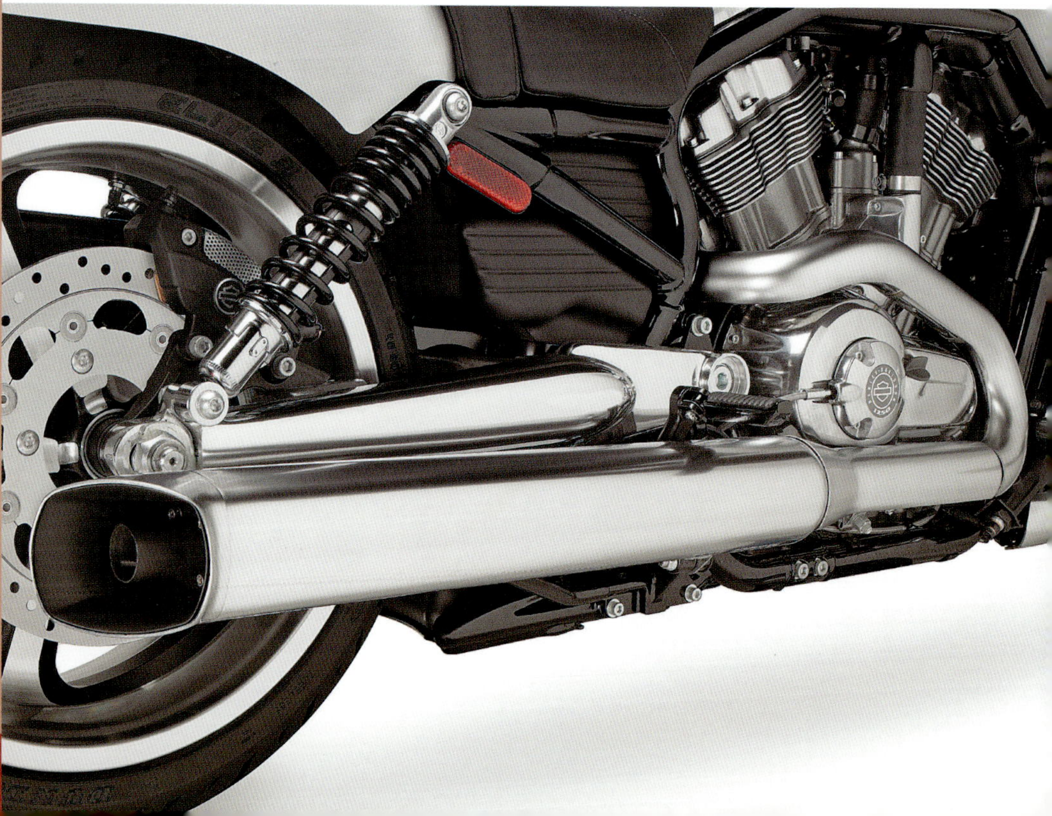

The name "Wide Glide" has graced some of Harley-Davidson's most memorable motorcycles. The first version, introduced in 1980, with its "bobtail" rear fender, forward foot controls, wide 41mm front forks with extended tubes, flamed 5-gallon gas tank (with center instrument panel), and staggered shorty exhausts, came closer to replicating the look of the radical custom chopped motorcycles of the day than had any factory custom yet. The original Wide

2010 FXDWG WIDE GLIDE

Price: $14,499
Torque: 92 lb-ft @ 3,000 rpm
Engine Displacement: 96 cubic inches
Engine Bore & Stroke: 3.75 x 4.38 inches
Weight: 647 pounds
Wheelbase: 68.3 inches
Wheel Size (F/R): 21/17 inches
Tire Size (F/R): 80/90-21/180/17
Seat Height: 25.5 inches
Number Produced: NA

Glide proved popular—Harley-Davidson sold 6,085 examples in 1980. One of those originals went to millionaire capitalist Malcolm Forbes, who traveled around the world aboard his Wide Glide.

The Wide Glide name has come and gone and come again over the years. After a brief hiatus, the Dyna-framed version, which originally debuted in 1993, has reappeared in the Harley lineup for 2010. Today's version captures the excitement of the original, right down to the optional flame paint scheme, but in place of the original's 80-cubic-inch Shovelhead engine, today's version gets its motivation from a 96-cubic-inch Twin Cam that cranks out an astounding 92 lb-ft of torque. This is a thoroughly modern engine, with electronic sequential port fuel injection as standard equipment. This is mated to a six-speed transmission that generates its power to the rear wheel by a clean, quiet, smooth, and reliable belt drive system.

If the optional flame paint doesn't provide enough excitement, the 2010 Wide Glide's list of standard features, like the two-into-one-into-two Tommy Gun exhaust system, drag-style handlebars, sissy bar, and side-mounted license plate adds plenty of spice.

Somewhere in Harley heaven, Wide Glide fan Malcolm Forbes must be smiling.

Did You Know?
Before Harley produced a factory version of the Wide Glide, customers created their own versions by stripping the chrome shrouds from the forks of FL touring bikes and mounting them on FX cruisers.

INDEX